MW00508257

THE IMPERIAL INSTITUTE

OF

THE UNITED KINGDOM, THE COLONIES, AND INDIA.

FOUNDED AND INCORPORATED BY ROYAL CHARTER A.D. 1887, AS
THE NATIONAL MEMORIAL OF QUEEN VICTORIA'S JUBILEE.

Patron.
HER MAJESTY THE QUEEN AND EMPRESS.

President.
H.R.H. THE PRINCE OF WALES, K.G.

SECOND EDITION.

IMPERIAL INSTITUTE ROAD, LONDON, S.W.

1893.

[Issued under the authority of the Executive Council.]

CONTENTS.

I N D E X.

THE GOVERNING BODY.

President.

H.R.H. THE PRINCE OF WALES, K.G., &c., &c., &c.

Governors.

THE RIGHT HON. THE LORD HERSCHELL, D.C.L., F.R.S.
(THE LORD CHANCELLOR), CHAIRMAN.

(*Governors nominated by the Sovereign.*)

His GRACE the DUKE OF FIFE, K.T.
The Most Noble the MARQUIS OF SALISBURY K.G., D.C.L., LL.D.
The Rt. Hon. the EARL OF ROSEBERY, K.G., LL.D., F.R.S., F.S.A.
The Rt. Hon. LORD CARRINGTON, G.C.M.G.
The LORD ROTHSCHILD.
The Rt. Hon. LORD HERSCHELL, D.C.L., F.R.S. (The Lord Chancellor).
The LORD THRING, K.C.B.
The LORD IVEAGH.
The Rt. Hon. LORD PLAYFAIR, K.C.B., F.R.S., LL.D.
The Rt. Hon. SIR HENRY JAMES, Q.C., M.P.
SIR JOHN STRACHEY, G.C.S.I., C.I.E.
Major-Gen. SIR OWEN TUDOR BURNE, K.C.S.I., C.I.E.

(*Governors nominated by H.R.H. the President.*)

The Rt. Hon. the LORD KNUTSFORD, G.C.M.G.
The Rt. Hon. HENRY H. FOWLER, M.P.
The Rt. Hon. WILLIAM LIDDERDALE.
THOMAS BURT, ESQ., M.P.
AUGUSTUS WILLIAM GADESDEN, ESQ.
JOHN HOLLAMS, ESQ. (*Honorary Solicitor*).

To represent the Islands of the British Seas.

The MARQUIS OF LORNE, K.T., G.C.M.G.

(Ex-officio Governors under the Constitution.)

The ARCHBISHOP OF CANTERBURY.
The LORD HIGH CHANCELLOR OF ENGLAND.
The SPEAKER OF THE HOUSE OF COMMONS.
The CHAIRMAN OF THE LONDON COUNTY COUNCIL.
The LORD MAYOR OF LONDON.
The LORD PROVOST OF EDINBURGH.
The LORD MAYOR OF DUBLIN.
The GOVERNOR OF THE BANK OF ENGLAND.

(Governors appointed to represent the Colonies.)

By the Governments of—

THE DOMINION OF CANADA—The Hon. SIR CHARLES TUPPER, Bart., G.C.M.G., C.B. (*High Commissioner in London for the Dominion of Canada*).

The Province of Ontario—SIR HENRY TYLER, and JOHN RAE, Esq., M.D., LL.D., F.R.S., F.R.G.S.

The Province of Quebec—SIR DONALD A. SMITH, K.C.M.G., and J. S. HALL, Esq.

The Province of Nova Scotia—The Hon. W. S. FIELDING (*Premier*).

The Province of New Brunswick—JAMES J. FELLOWS, Esq.

The Province of Prince Edward Island.—DONALD FARQUHARSON, Esq.

The Province of Manitoba—The Rt. Hon. the EARL OF ABERDEEN.

The North-West Territories—PETER REDPATH, Esq.

The Province of British Columbia—HENRY COPPINGER BEETON, Esq. (*Agent General*).

THE COLONIES OR SETTLEMENTS OF—

New South Wales—SIR SAUL SAMUEL, K.C.M.G., C.B. (*Agent General*), and SIR DANIEL COOPER, Bart., G.C.M.G.

Victoria—HOWARD SPENSLEY, Esq., and SIR ANDREW CLARKE (*temporary*).

Queensland—SIR THOMAS MacILWRAITH, K.C.M.G., and SIR JAMES GARRICK, K.C.M.G. (*Agent General*).

South Australia—SIR JOHN COX BRAY, K.C.M.G. (*Agent General*), and HENRY BULL TEMPLAR STRANGWAYS, Esq.

Western Australia—The AGENT GENERAL for the time being (SIR MALCOLM FRASER, K.C.M.G.).

Tasmania—THE AGENT GENERAL—SIR E. BRADDON, K.C.M.G. (*ex officio*).

New Zealand—SIR WALTER L. BULLER, K.C.M.G., and WESTBY B. PERCEVAL, Esq. (*Agent General*).

Cape Colony—The Rt. Hon. SIR HERCULES G. R. ROBINSON, G.C.M.G., and SIR CHARLES MILLS, K.C.M.G., C.B. (*Agent General*).

Newfoundland—AUSTIN R. WHITEWAY, Esq., Barrister-at-Law.

British Guiana, Trinidad, and Tobago—SIR ARTHUR HAMILTON GORDON, G.C.M.G.

Ceylon—Vacant by death.

Gibraltar, Malta, Cyprus, Bermuda, Fiji and Falkland Islands—Field-Marshal SIR JOHN LINTORN ARABIN SIMMONS, G.C.B., G.C.M.G.

Hong Kong—The Rt. Hon. SIR GEORGE F. BOWEN, G.C.M.G.

Jamaica, British Honduras, and Bahamas—CHARLES WASHINGTON EVES, Esq., C.M.G.

The Leeward Islands, The Windward Islands, and Barbados—Sir RAWSON WILLIAM RAWSON, K.C.M.G., C.B.

Mauritius—H. J. JOURDAIN, Esq., C.M.G.

Natal—WILLIAM DUNN, Esq., M.P. (W. DUNN & Co.).

The Straits Settlements—Lt.-General SIR W. F. DRUMMOND JERVOIS, R.E., G.C.M.G., C.B.

The West African Colonies and St. Helena—SIR SANFORD FREELING, K.C.M.G.

(*Governors appointed to represent India.*)

THE GOVERNMENT OF INDIA—

W. T. THISELTON DYER, Esq., C.M.G., F.R.S. (Director of Kew Gardens); General JAMES T. WALKER, R.E., C.B., LL.D. (late Surveyor-General of India); Doctor GEORGE WATT, C.I.E. (Reporter on Economic Products to the Government of India).

PROVINCES AND NATIVE STATES—

Bombay—SIR RAYMOND WEST, K.C.I.E.

Madras—DAVID F. CARMICHAEL, Esq. (late Madras Civil Service).

Bengal—SIR ALFRED WOODLEY CROFT, K.C.I.E.

North-West Provinces and Oudh—W. S. HALSEY, Esq. (formerly of the Bengal Civil Service).

Punjab—BADEN H. BADEN-POWELL, Esq., C.I.E. (late Bengal Civil Service).

Jeypur—Surgeon-Lt.-Col. T. H. HENDLEY, C.I.E. (Residency Surgeon, Jeypur).

INDIAN CHAMBERS OF COMMERCE—

Bombay—SIR FRANK FORBES ADAM, C.I.E. (of Messrs. Graham & Co., Manchester).

Rangoon—JOHN ANNAN BRYCE, Esq. (of Messrs. Wallace Brothers).

Madras—GEORGE G. ARBUTHNOT, Esq.

Calcutta—SIR ALEXANDER WILSON (of Messrs. Matheson & Co., London).

INDIAN INSTITUTIONS—

Bombay—DADABHAI NAOROJI, Esq., M.P.

Bengal—SIR WILLIAM WILSON HUNTER, K.C.S.I., C.I.E.

(*Governors elected by County and Municipal Authorities of Great Britain.*)

South-Eastern District of England—The Rt. Hon. EARL OF SANDWICH and R. D. M. LITTLER, Esq., C.B., Q.C.

South-Western District of England—The Rt. Hon. EARL OF DUCIE and SIR HENRY JOHN WARING.

Midland District of England—FREDERICK. ELKINGTON, Esq., J.P., and the Rt. Hon. VISCOUNT OXENBRIDGE.

Cheshire and Lancashire—SIR WILLIAM HOULDSWORTH, Bart., M.P., and the Right Hon. JOHN T. HIBBERT.

Yorkshire—ANGUS HOLDEN, Esq., M.P., and ALDERMAN J. F. WOODHOUSE.

Northern District of England—SIR LOWTHIAN BELL, Bart., D.C.L., F.R.S., and SIR BENJAMIN CHAPMAN BROWNE, D.C.L.

North Wales—STUART RENDEL, Esq., M.P.

South Wales—SIR HENRY HUSSEY VIVIAN, Bart., M.P.

South-East Scotland—The Most Noble the MARQUIS OF LOTHIAN, K.T., LL.D.

South-West Scotland—SIR JOHN MUIR, of Deanstone, Bart.

North Scotland—The Rt. Hon. VISCOUNT STORMONT.

(Governors elected by County and Municipal and Commercial Authorities of Ireland.)

Elected by the Lord Mayor of Dublin and certain Mayors and Chairmen of Town Commissioners—ALDERMAN CONNOR and ALDERMAN HORGAN.

Elected by the Chairmen of certain Chambers of Commerce—JAMES MUSGRAVE, Esq., J.P., and MICHAEL MURPHY, Esq., J.P.

(Governors appointed to represent Commercial, Scientific, and Artistic Associations and Institutions.)

The Associated Chambers of Commerce of the United Kingdom—THE PRESIDENT (now Sir ALBERT KAYE ROLLIT, LL.D., M.P.) and the SENIOR VICE-PRESIDENT OF THE ASSOCIATION (now T. F. FIRTH, Esq.) (*ex-officio*).

The London Chamber of Commerce—SIR ALBERT KAYE ROLLIT, LL.D., M.P. (Chairman).

The Royal Agricultural Society of England—THE PRESIDENT (*ex-officio*) [now the EARL OF FEVERSHAM].

The Central Chamber of Agriculture—THE CHAIRMAN (*ex-officio*).

The Highland and Agricultural Society of Scotland—H.R.H. THE DUKE OF YORK, K.G. (President).

The Royal Society—PROFESSOR AYRTON, F.R.S. (to hold office so long as he remains a Fellow of the Royal Society).

The Royal Society of Edinburgh—THE PRESIDENT (now SIR DOUGLAS MACLAGAN, M.D., F.R.C.P., F.R.S.) (*ex-officio*.)

The Royal Irish Academy—DR. JOHN KELLS INGRAM (The President).

The Royal Dublin Society—THE PRESIDENT (who is also Chairman of the Council) [now the VISCOUNT POWERSCOURT, K.P.] (*ex-officio*).

The Society for the Encouragement of Arts, Manufactures, and Commerce—THE CHAIRMAN OF COUNCIL (now SIR RICHARD WEBSTER, Q.C., M.P.).

The Institution of Civil Engineers—THE PRESIDENT (now HARRISON HAYTER, Esq., 25, Great George Street, Westminster, London, S.W.) (*ex-officio*).

The Institution of Mechanical Engineers—THE PRESIDENT [now Dr. WILLIAM ANDERSON, F.R.S.] (*ex-officio*).

The Iron and Steel Institute—SIR JAMES KITSON, Bart. (Past President).

The Chemical Society of London—PROFESSOR H. E. ARMSTRONG, F.R.S.

The Society of Chemical Industry—E. RIDER COOK, Esq.

The Institution of Electrical Engineers—THE PRESIDENT (now WILLIAM H. PREECE, Esq., F.R.S.).

The City and Guilds of London Institute for the advancement of Technical Education—JOHN WATNEY, Esq. (*the Honorary Secretary*).

The Royal United Service Institution—ADMIRAL SIR GEORGE WILLES, G.C.B. (Chairman of Council).

The Royal Academy of Arts—SIR FREDERICK LEIGHTON, Bart., P.R.A.

The Royal Geographical Society—THE RIGHT HONOURABLE SIR MOUNTSTUART E. GRANT DUFF, G.C.S.I., C.I.E., F.R.S.

The Royal Statistical Society—THE PRESIDENT (*ex-officio*).

The Royal Institute of British Architects—THE PRESIDENT (*ex-officio*).

The Mining Association of Great Britain—ARTHUR MARSHALL CHAMBERS, Esq. (President).

The Trades Union Congress of Great Britain—EDWARD HARFORD, Esq.

The National Miners' Union of Great Britain—JOHN WILSON, Esq., M.P. (Secretary).

TRUSTEES OF THE IMPERIAL INSTITUTE.

THE DUKE OF FIFE, K.T.
THE EARL OF ROSEBERY, K.G.
THE LORD HERSCHELL.

THE EXECUTIVE COUNCIL.

LORD HERSCHELL (The Lord Chancellor), Chairman (*ex-officio*).

*Sir Lowthian Bell.
Sir Owen Tudor Burne.
Mr. T. Burt, M.P.
Lord Carrington.
Alderman Connor.
Mr. W. Crookes.
Mr. C. Washington Eves.
The Duke of Fife.
Rt. Hon. H. H. Fowler.
Mr. A. W. Gadesden.
Sir James Garrick.
*Mr. Angus Holden.
Mr. John Hollams.
Lord Iveagh.
Sir Henry James.

Lord Knutsford.
Sir Frederick Leighton.
The Marquis of Lothian.
*Sir Charles Mills.
*Mr. Dadabhai Naoroji.
Lord Playfair of St. Andrews.
The Earl of Rosebery.
Sir Saul Samuel.
The Earl of Sandwich.
*Sir Lintorn Simmons.
Sir John Strachey.
Lord Thring.
Sir Charles Tupper.
Sir Richard Webster.
*Sir Alexander Wilson.

* *Nominated by His Royal Highness the President.*

Secretary and Director.
SIR FREDERICK A. ABEL, K.C.B., F.R.S., D.C.L., D.Sc.

Assistant Secretary and General Sub-Director.
SIR J. R. SOMERS VINE, F.R.G.S., F.S.S.

Chief Clerk.
MR. CLAUDE JOHNSON.

Accountant.
MR. G. F. DICKIE.

Honorary Solicitor.
MR. JOHN HOLLAMS (of Messrs. Hollams, Sons & Coward).

Honorary Surveyor.
MR. ROBERT VIGERS (of Messrs. Vigers & Co., 4, Fredericks Place, Old Jewry).

Bankers.
THE BANK OF ENGLAND,
and
THE LONDON AND WESTMINSTER BANK, Lothbury, E.C.

Auditors.
MESSRS. LOVELOCK, H. S. WHIFFIN & DICKINSON, 19, Coleman Street, E.C.

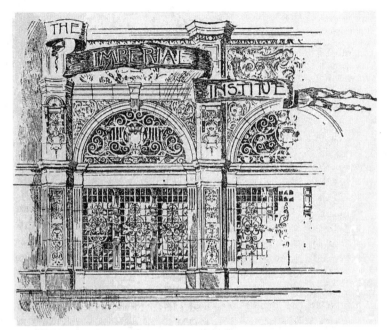

ORNAMENTAL SCREENS IN THE MAIN ENTRANCE OF THE INSTITUTE.

THE ORIGIN OF THE IMPERIAL INSTITUTE, AND THE COURSE OF ITS ORGANISATION AND DEVELOPMENT FROM 1887 TO 1893.

THE great interest excited throughout the British Empire by the display at the Colonial and Indian Exhibition of 1886, which illustrated the vast wealth in natural products, and the commercial, industrial, artistic and educational achievements of our various Colonies and of India, led His Royal Highness the Prince of Wales to suggest that a permanent Institution, designed to afford a thorough and living representation of the progress made in the development of their resources, and elaborated upon a scale commensurate with the importance of their relations to the prosperity of the Empire, might constitute a fitting National Memorial commemorative of the fiftieth year of the reign of Her Majesty, an epoch within which some of our most important and thriving Colonies passed from insignificance and even comparative barbarism to exalted positions in the commercial and civilized world.

This valuable suggestion became the germ of the proposal to establish an Imperial Institute, designed not only to illustrate the industrial and commercial resources of the Colonies and India, and to diffuse a knowledge of their present condition and continued progress throughout the United Kingdom, but also to afford to all classes of Her Majesty's subjects opportunities of becoming acquainted with the development, during the Queen's reign, and with the further extension from time to time, of the resources, natural, industrial, and commercial, of the United Kingdom itself, and, by actively promoting technical and higher commercial education, to advance the industrial and commercial prosperity of the country.

With these objects in view the Prince of Wales, on the 13th of September, 1886, addressed a letter to the then Lord Mayor, the late Sir John Staples, K.C.M.G., of which the following are extracts :—

"My attention has been frequently called to the general anxiety that is felt to commemorate in some special manner the approaching Jubilee of Her Majesty's reign.

It appears to me that no more suitable memorial could be suggested than an Institute which should represent the Arts, Manufactures, and Commerce of the Empire.

Such an Institution would, it seems to me, be singularly appropriate to the occasion, for it would illustrate the progress already made during Her Majesty's reign in the Colonial and Indian Dominions, while it would record year by year the development of the Empire in the Arts of Civilization.

It would thus be deeply interesting to Her Majesty's subjects, both within and beyond these Islands, and would tend to stimulate Emigration to those British territories where it is required, to expand the trade between the different British Communities, and to draw closer the bonds which unite the Empire.

It would be at once a Museum, an Exhibition, and the proper locality for the discussion of Colonial and Indian subjects.

*　*　*　*　*　*　*　*

I have much satisfaction in addressing this letter to your Lordship as Chief Magistrate of the Capital of the Empire, and invite your co-operation in the formation of this Imperial Institute as the Memorial of Her Majesty's Jubilee by Her subjects.

Should your Lordship concur in this proposal, and be willing to open a fund at the Mansion House, I would suggest that the contributions received be vested in a body of Trustees, and I would further suggest that the Institution should be under the permanent Presidency of the Heir Apparent to the Throne."

To this communication the Lord Mayor replied in the following terms :—

"I have the honour to acknowledge the receipt of your Royal Highness's letter of the 13th inst., and in reply, to express the great pleasure it will afford me to give the heartiest co-operation and aid in the formation of the proposed Imperial Institute as the Memorial of Her Majesty's Jubilee by Her subjects.

Your Royal Highness truly states that general anxiety is felt to commemorate in some special manner the approaching Jubilee of Her Majesty's Reign. There will, I am sure, be an universal desire to give expression, in a suitable and, if possible, adequate way to the deep attachment, veneration, and loyalty which the Queen's subjects in all parts of Her vast dominions entertain for a Sovereign, whose long and illustrious reign has been productive, under Providence, of many blessings to Her people, and been rendered memorable by the striking progress in civilization and prosperity developed throughout the Empire.

Difficult as it may be to signalise in a commensurate way the feelings which are thus naturally emphasised at the approach of the Jubilee of Her Majesty's Reign, I am convinced that the proposal which your Royal Highness indicates, and which has the support of your influence, will be considered singularly appropriate.

It will, therefore, give me much satisfaction to open a Fund at the Mansion House for the receipt of contributions, as suggested by Your Royal Highness."

The next step taken by the Prince of Wales was to appoint a Committee of Organisation, which included the under-mentioned noblemen and gentlemen :—Lord Herschell (Chairman), the late Earl of Carnarvon, Lords Revelstoke, Rothschild, and Knutsford, Sir Lyon Playfair, Sir Henry James, Mr. Goschen, Mr. H. H. Fowler, Mr. Ritchie, Sir Frederick Leighton, the late Sir Ashley Eden, Sir Owen Burne, Sir Frederick Abel, the Lord Mayor, the Governor of the Bank of England, the President of the London Chamber of Commerce, Mr. Henry Broadhurst, and Mr. Neville Lubbock. A small working staff was also formed, and Sir Frederick Abel and Sir Somers Vine were appointed by the Prince of Wales as Organising Secretary and Assistant-Secretary respectively.

The first duty of the Organising Committee was to frame the scheme for an Imperial Institute, and a Report was prepared and published by that Body, on the 20th December, 1886, setting forth the outline of a proposal for harmoniously combining, with a view to the attainment of objects of practical and enduring utility, a representation of the Colonies and India, on the one hand, and of the United Kingdom on the other.

The issue of this Report was immediately followed by active measures for the collection of subscriptions throughout the

Empire for the establishment and maintenance of the Imperial
Institute, whereby, before the end of·the year 1887, promises of
contributions amounting to nearly £350,000 had been secured.
At the beginning of 1893 the donations received gave a total of
£400,352; those promised, but not transmitted, amounted to
£12,500, thus bringing the full value of the Subscription List to
about £413,000.

The following is a statement of the amounts contributed by
the United Kingdom, the Indian Empire, and the Colonies :—

	Official Donations.		Private Donations.		Total.	
	£	s.	£	s.	£	s.
United Kingdom	...		236,862	0	236,862	0
India..	...		101,550	0	101,550	0
Dominion of Canada	20,000	0	87	0	20,087	0
Colonies or Settlements of—						
Victoria	5,922	0	5,397	0	11,319	0
Straits Settlements	5,000	0	3,581	0	8,581	0
New South Wales	5,915	0	...		5,915	0
New Zealand	...		2,853	0	2,853	0
South Australia	1,845	0	368	0	2,213	0
Queensland	2,029	0	68	0	2,097	0
Western Australia	2,000	0	...		2,000	0
British Guiana...	1,000	0	204	0	1,204	0
Bermuda	1,000	0	...		1,000	0
Jamaica	1,000	0	25	0	1,025	0
Tasmania	1,000	0	...		1,000	0
Trinidad	1,000	0	...		1,000	0
British Honduras	746	0	...		746	0
Ceylon	...		648	0	648	0
Cape Colony	...		535	0	535	0
Lagos	500	0	...		500	0
Gibraltar	200	0	100	0	300	0
Falkland Islands	...		255	0	255	0
Bahamas	150	0	70	0	220	0
Barbados			137	0	137	0
Natal			112	0	112	0
Gold Coast	...		108	0	108	0
Cyprus	...		100	0	100	0
Labuan...	...		75	0	75	0
Fiji	...		46	0	46	0
Leeward Islands	...		33	0	33	0
St. Lucia	...		22	0	22	0
Ascension	...		1	10	1	10

The private subscribers include fifty-eight Foundation Donors
of £500 and upwards, and nearly five hundred contributors of
not less than £50 each. The subscription lists sent in from
different parts of the country comprised individual donations
varying from ten thousand pounds to one penny. The total

number of subscribers, belonging as they did to every class of the Queen's subjects, amounts to several millions.

The particulars here given do not include the financial arrangements made or being made by several of the Colonies for establishing the collections to be displayed, and providing for their guardianship and annual maintenance. The following is an outline of the special arrangements now in operation :—

Collections of products have already been prepared and transmitted by the Governments of India, Ceylon, Straits Settlements, and Mauritius ; the Canadian provinces : of Quebec, Ontario, British Columbia, and Manitoba ; Victoria, Queensland, Tasmania, West Coast of Africa, Zanzibar, Cape Colony, Natal, Hong-Kong, and Malta.

Collections of products are in course of preparation and transmission by the Governments of New South Wales, South Australia, West Australia, British Guiana, the Windward Islands, the Leeward Islands, British Honduras, Bahamas, Bermuda, Malta, the Canadian province of New Brunswick and the North West Territories, and the Falkland Islands.

Cases and Fittings for their respective sections have been provided by the Governments of India, Ceylon, the Straits Settlements, Hong-Kong, and Mauritius ; the Canadian provinces of Quebec, Ontario, British Columbia, and Manitoba ; British Guiana, New South Wales, Victoria, Queensland, and New Guinea, South Australia, West Australia, Tasmania, New Zealand, Cape Colony, and Natal. Those for Jamaica and the Canadian province of New Brunswick have been provided by the munificence of their representatives on the Governing Body of the Institute.

Curators and Officers in charge of Collections have been appointed by the Governments of India, Ceylon, the Canadian provinces, New South Wales, Victoria, Cape Colony, and Jamaica.

Conference Rooms have been furnished and fitted for British America (Canada) by the Governments of the Canadian provinces ; for British Australasia by the Governments of New South Wales, Victoria, Queensland, South Australia, West Australia, Tasmania, and New Zealand ; for British Africa

by the Governments of the Cape Colony and Natal; for
the Eastern Crown Colonies by the Governments of the Straits
Settlements, Mauritius, Sierra Leone, Gold Coast, Gambia,
Gibraltar, Malta, Ceylon, and the British North Borneo
Company in respect of Labuan; and for the Western Crown
Colonies by the Governments of Trinidad, Jamaica, Barbados,
British Honduras, Granada, St. Vincent, St. Lucia, Bahamas, and
the Falkland Islands.

A Permanent Endowment Fund has been, by the powers
contained in the charter of incorporation, appropriated from the
public subscriptions, and is vested in three trustees (the Duke
of Fife, the Earl of Rosebery, and Lord Herschell). It originally
stood at £141,520, and produced an annual income of £4,000; but
of this sum £26,000 has, by decision of the Executive Council,
been applied to the erection of the North Gallery, the upper floor
of which is permanently leased to Her Majesty's Government at
a rental equivalent to three per centum on the sum thus expended.

On the 12th January, 1887, the Prince of Wales presided,
at St. James's Palace, over an assembly which included representatives of county, municipal, and other local authorities of
the United Kingdom; the presidents, secretaries, and other
officers of the most prominent scientific, commercial, artistic, and
technical institutions and associations of the country, and the
leading home-representatives of the Colonies and India. At this
meeting resolutions approving of the proposals set forth in the
Report of the Organising Committee were unanimously adopted.
A very numerously attended public meeting was held at the
Mansion House on the same day, when resolutions were passed
similar to those adopted at the meeting at St. James's Palace.

In the early part of 1887, the objects of the Institute were
publicly disseminated by the extensive distribution, throughout
the Empire, of brief summaries of the main objects of the
Institute, and also of an address delivered at the Royal Institution, on April 22nd, 1887, by Sir Frederick Abel, before His
Royal Highness the Prince of Wales and a numerous audience,
on "The Work of the Imperial Institute."

The foundation-stone of the Institute was laid by Her
Majesty the Queen, on the 4th of July, 1887, in the presence of

a brilliant assembly of more than 10,000 specially-invited spectators. This "foundation," or "corner-stone"—as our Trans-
atlantic brethren prefer to name it—is a huge block of granite
from Cape Colony, and stands on a pedestal of Indian bricks,
which in their turn cover a specially-prepared cavity containing
current coins of the realm and a number of documents of a
public character. The ceremony was attended by every auspi-
cious omen, and in the interest it excited it was second only
to that memorable ceremonial on Jubilee day, which closely
preceded it.

The main entrance to the temporary building where the
ceremony took place had served as the principal ingress to
the Colonial and Indian Exhibition in Exhibition Road. A
variegated awning had been erected over the pavement from the
door of the vestibule to the roadway. On crossing the threshold
of this entrance, the visitors passed through what may fitly be
described as a garden of exotics. A grove of tall and spreading
palms had been transplanted into the broad area of the vestibule,
where was displayed a great trophy of Indian and Colonial
flags, surmounted by the Union Jack, the folds of which reached
from the ceiling. In the centre of this vestibule stood the copy
of Boehm's equestrian statue of the Prince of Wales, which
had been the first object to attract the attention of the
multitudes who had visited the Exhibitions from 1883 to 1886,
and which was a fitting reminder, had such been needed, of
the moving spirit in the foundation of the Imperial Institute.
Retiring rooms of Oriental character had been erected on the
right-hand side of the main entrance, for the accommodation of
the Queen and the other royal personages. From the vestibule
the visitors passed down a corridor leading by a winding route
to the gigantic pavilion which accommodated nearly eleven
thousand persons, without inconvenience of any kind. In shape,
an oblong with semicircular ends, it presented somewhat of
the appearance of a huge amphitheatre, with an arena nearly
200 feet in length, and more than 60 in width. Thirty tiers
of seats rose from the arena, and these, with the floor and
daïs, were clothed in scarlet cloth. The daïs, which stood
almost in the centre of the arena, had a canopy covered

externally with scarlet silk; it was surmounted by a crown
upon a cushion, and had the Royal Arms and monogram in
front. It rested upon columns draped in white and scarlet,
several of which were surrounded at the base with groups of
flowers, concealing large blocks of ice designed to keep the
temperature of the daïs cool. The orchestra rose from behind
the daïs, and in front were several blocks of seats arranged in
a curve so as all to face the daïs, and reserved for some of the
more distinguished among the spectators, including the members
of the two Houses of Parliament. On the left of the daïs were
the seats of the members of the Organising Committee of the
Imperial Institute, and on the right those of the Royal
Commissioners of the Exhibition of 1851 (the donors of the site).
As the clock struck ten, the doors were opened and a continuous
stream of visitors arrived, until, without the occurrence of any
confusion, the vast pavilion was compactly filled.

The scene then presented was rendered the more imposing
to visitors in that it was possible to see over the whole
of the pavilion from every point of view. The band of the
Grenadier Guards, stationed on the upper tiers of the blocks
of seats in front of the daïs, performed a selection of music
during the assemblage of the visitors, under the direction of
Lieutenant Dan Godfrey. The Indian Princes who attended
the ceremony included the Rao of Kutch, Kumar Shri Kalooba
(brother of the Rao), the Maharaja and Maharani of Kuch
Behar, the Thakur Sahib of Morvi, the Thakur Sahib of Limri,
the Thakur Sahib of Gondal, K.C.I.E., the Maharaja Sir
Pertab Singh, K.C.S.I., Kunwar Harnam Singh, Ahluwalia,
C.I.E., of Kapurthalla, and Kanwarani Harnam Singh, the
Nawab Amir-i-Akbar Asman Jah Bahadur, Prime Minister to
the Nizam, the Nawab Zaffer Jung Shums-ud-Dowlah, the
Shums-ul-Moolk of Hyderabad, Sirdar Diler-ul-Moolk, C.I.E.
The native officers of the Indian cavalry were on duty at the
pavilion entrances, the Honourable Corps of Gentlemen-at-Arms
were stationed near the daïs, and the Yeomen of the Guard
were posted at the main entrance in the Exhibition Road.

The daïs was soon tenanted by Royal personages, among the
first to arrive being the Duke of Cambridge, the Prince and
Princess Christian, the King of Denmark, and the Crown Prince

and Princess of Portugal. Just after twelve o'clock there was a general movement of expectation in the pavilion, as the arrival of the Queen became known, and the entrance of Her Majesty was awaited with the keenest interest. As the procession entered the pavilion there was a flourish of trumpets, and the orchestra played a processional march under the direction of Sir Arthur Sullivan, while her Majesty and the Royal Family were taking their places on the daïs. The National Anthem was then sung by the Royal Albert Hall Choral Society and the pupils of the Royal College of Music, whereupon the Prince of Wales read to Her Majesty the following address on the part of the Organising Committee of the Imperial Institute :—

"May it please your Majesty—We, the President of the Imperial Institute and the Organising Committee appointed to advise upon the form and constitution of that memorial of the 50th anniversary of your Majesty's Accession to the Throne, approach your Majesty with the expression of our heartfelt affection and loyalty.

It has been our desire, in pursuance of the ideas which gave birth to the Colonial and Indian Exhibition of 1886, to combine in some harmonious form a broader and more enduring representation of your Majesty's Colonies and India as well as of the United Kingdom, and our confident hope is that this Institute may hereafter not only exhibit the material resources of the Empire, but may be an emblem of that Imperial unity of purpose and action which we believe has gathered strength and reality with every year of your Majesty's reign.

We would also express our hope that this Institution may promote the commercial and industrial prosperity of all parts of your Majesty's dominions, and that the scientific and technical education which the requirements of modern industry render necessary may, through its means, receive fresh development.

In praying your Majesty to associate yourself with this work, we trust that we shall not err if we venture to remind your Majesty of yet one more consideration which may enhance your Majesty's personal interest in this undertaking, even if we refer to a never-forgotten sorrow.

More than 36 years ago, under the counsel and wise guidance of your Majesty's illustrious and lamented Consort, my beloved father, the Exhibition of 1851 gave a vast impulse to commercial activity, and set an example which has been often followed in the countries both of the old and of the new worlds. The creation of an Imperial Institute would seem to be a fitting development and completion of the work thus wisely and usefully initiated.

The financial success of that great and bold enterprise has enabled your Majesty's Commissioners to grant this site for the purposes of this Institute, and thus to render the entire fund contributed by your Majesty's subjects directly available for its erection and maintenance.

In this tribute of love and loyalty every class and race, every colony and country that owns your Majesty's beneficent sway will take part, and in it they will see a record of those 50 years of public progress and prosperity which will make your Majesty's reign famous in English history.

It is our earnest hope that the building, of which your Majesty to-day lays the foundation-stone, will tell to many generations yet to come the story of the long and happy reign of our gracious Sovereign."

Her Majesty then read the following reply, which was handed to her by the Secretary of State for the Home Department :—

"It is with infinite satisfaction that I receive the address in which you give expression to your loyal attachment to my throne and person, and develop the views that have led to the creation of the Imperial Institute.

I concur with you in thinking that the counsels and exertions of my beloved husband initiated a movement which gave increased vigour to commercial activity, and produced marked and lasting improvements in industrial efforts.

One indirect result of that movement has been to bring more before the minds of men the vast and varied resources of the Empire over which Providence has willed that I should reign during 50 prosperous years.

I believe and hope that the Imperial Institute will play a useful part in combining those resources for the common advantage of all my subjects, and in conducing towards the welding of the Colonies, India, and the Mother Country into one harmonious and united community.

In laying the foundation-stone of the building devoted to your labours, I heartily wish you God speed in your undertaking."

At the conclusion of Her Majesty's reply an Ode, written for the occasion by Mr. Lewis Morris, and set to music by Sir Arthur Sullivan, was performed under the conductorship of the latter by the Royal Albert Hall Choral Society, and a full orchestra, assisted by the pupils of the Royal College of Music.

At the conclusion of the Ode, Her Majesty advanced to the spot where the stone was to be laid, and the Prince of Wales handed to her a statement of the origin of the Institute, together with a collection of the coins of the year. These, with the assistance of the Prince, Her Majesty deposited beneath the stone. His Royal Highness then handed the silver trowel and ivory gavel to the Queen, who proceeded to lay the foundation-stone.

Prayer having been offered, the Commissioners of the Exhibition of 1851 presented an address of congratulation to the Queen, on the attainment of the Jubilee of Her reign. The proceedings concluded with a benediction, pronounced by the Archbishop of Canterbury, and the Queen left the pavilion on the arm of the Prince of Wales, "Rule Britannia" being played and sung as Her Majesty was conducted to her carriage, amid the cheers of the audience.

From first to last the pageant formed a gorgeous and a memorable picture. As the eye roved from end to end of that great amphitheatre, and fell upon the many tiers of spectators, the mind unconsciously reverted to the Jubilee thanksgiving in Westminster Abbey; the ceremonial of the day was felt, by all who witnessed it, to be a happy sequel and a fitting complement to that historic scene. But it was more than this; it was a contrast also. In the one case the prevailing sentiment was one of retrospection, in the other it was one of hopeful anticipation; and so the scene, although brilliant, and in itself imposing, was fraught with an interest far deeper and more abiding than any that pertains to mere spectacular magnificence, symbolic as it was of the fact that the triumphs of peace have contributed far more than those of war to the greatness of the British Empire.

On the 12th May, 1888, Her Majesty granted a Charter of ✝
Incorporation to the " Imperial Institute of the United Kingdom,
the Colonies and India, and the Isles of the British Seas," which
provided that, before the expiration of three years from the date
of the Charter, the Organising Committee should prepare a
form of constitution for the Institute, providing, amongst other
things, for such a Governing Body as, in their opinion, would
best represent Her Majesty's subjects in the United Kingdom,
the Colonies and India, and the commercial and industrial
interests of the Empire.

Lord Herschell, Chairman of the Governing Body, when
visiting India in the autumn of 1888, gave explanations of the
objects of the Imperial Institute to members of the Government
of India and of Provincial Governments and Associations, and
conferred with them on the subjects of supply to the Institute of
collections illustrating the natural and industrial resources of
different parts of India, and of arrangements for the regular
transmission of reliable intelligence of commercial interest. The
Government of India has since taken active measures for secur-
ing the preparation and future maintenance of very complete
collections of the natural products of India, and the regular
transmission of information regarding the extent and cost of
available supplies, and on other matters of commercial and
industrial importance. The Trustees of the National Museum
of Calcutta have been charged by the Government of India with
the work of preparing the collections, in communication with
the Revenue and Agricultural Department.

Towards the close of 1888, the Assistant Secretary, Sir
Somers Vine, was despatched on a mission to the principal
Colonies, upon the duties of which he was engaged during the
greater part of 1889 and 1890, having visited in those years
India and the Straits Settlements, the several Australasian
Colonies, the various Provinces of Canada, and most of the West
Indian and African Colonies. The authorities and commercial
bodies in the Colonies were thereby made acquainted with the
objects of the Imperial Institute ; the interest thus aroused
therein was demonstrated by the promises of practical co-
operation which were received on all sides. A reference to page
17 will denote those Colonies which are already acting up to

those promises by entering upon the work of preparation and transmission of collections.

A special Committee, consisting of Lord Herschell, Lord Thring, Sir Henry James, Sir Frederick Abel and Mr. Hollams, was occupied in 1889 and 1890 with the drafting of a form of constitution, which was adopted by the Organising Committee at a meeting held at Marlborough House, under the presidency of His Royal Highness the Prince of Wales, on the 5th March, and was approved by Royal Warrant on the 21st April, 1891 ; it deals comprehensively with the mode of election of the Governing Body, the appointment of Committees, the procedure at meetings, and the various points likely to arise thereon.

In accordance with the provisions embodied in the constitution, the several Colonial authorities and the Indian Government were requested, in 1890, to nominate their representatives to serve upon the Governing Body. The County Councils and leading Municipalities comprised within the several electoral districts, into which the United Kingdom has been divided for the purposes of the Imperial Institute, were invited in 1891 by the Prince of Wales to meet and to appoint their representatives ; and the various institutions and societies entitled to be represented upon the Governing Body were also called upon to forward the names of their representatives. The composition of the Governing Body and the particulars of the nominating authorities will be found at pages 7 to 11.

Regulations were also prescribed by the Special Committee and embodied in the constitution, with respect to the election, subscriptions and privileges of Fellows of the Institute.* (See page 51.)

The concluding meeting of the Organising Committee and the first meeting of the new Governing Body were held under the presidency of His Royal Highness the Prince of Wales, at Marlborough House, on the 23rd of July, 1891.

The first Meeting of the Executive Council was held on the 29th July, 1891, in the Council Chamber of the Imperial Institute Buildings, under the presidency of Lord Herschell, Chairman of the Governing Body.

The first Annual Meeting of the Governors and Fellows of the Institute, under the provisions of the Charter and Constitu-

---

* *The latter have been recently added to (see p. 55).*

tion, took place in the Executive Council Chamber at the
Institute, on Saturday, November 26th, 1892, His Royal Highness the Prince of Wales, President, being in the Chair. The
number of Fellowships at that time was reported as follows :—

Honorary Life Fellows	2
Foundation Life Fellows (Subscribers of not less than £500)	57
Chartered Life Fellows	37
Life Fellows (Subscribers of not less than £50)	462
Compounding Ordinary Fellows	316
Annually Subscribing Ordinary Fellows	3243
	4117*

In 1887 it was suggested that a school of Modern Oriental
Studies should be organised as a branch of the Institute, in
imitation of the very efficient establishments of this kind which
are carried on, with Government resources, in France,. Germany,
and Austria. The promulgation of this proposal led to nego-
tiations with the authorities of University College and King's
College, London, which resulted in their co-operation with the
Institute in the establishment of the School. A Special Committee having been appointed to decide upon a system of work,
it was arranged that classes for instruction in the Oriental
languages required by students qualifying for examinations
for the Indian Civil Service, should be held at University
College, while modern Oriental languages, other than the
Indian languages, should be taught at King's College, and that
the Imperial Institute should undertake the general administrative and financial work. The School was officially opened
in January, 1890, when an inaugural address was delivered by
Professor Max Müller at the Royal Institution, in the presence
of His Royal Highness the Prince of Wales. The daughters
of the late Colonel W. J. Ouseley (Bengal Army) have established and endowed, in his memory, three scholarships, in
Arabic and Persian, in connection with the School, each one of
the value of not less than £50 per annum. Other endowments
in connection with the School are contemplated.

---

* On the 31st of March, 1893, the numbers were as follows :—

Honorary Life Fellows	4
Foundation Life Fellows (£500 and upwards)	58
Chartered Life Fellows	38
Life Fellows (£50 and upwards)	464
Compounding Ordinary Fellows	537
Annually Subscribing Ordinary Fellows	5173
	6274

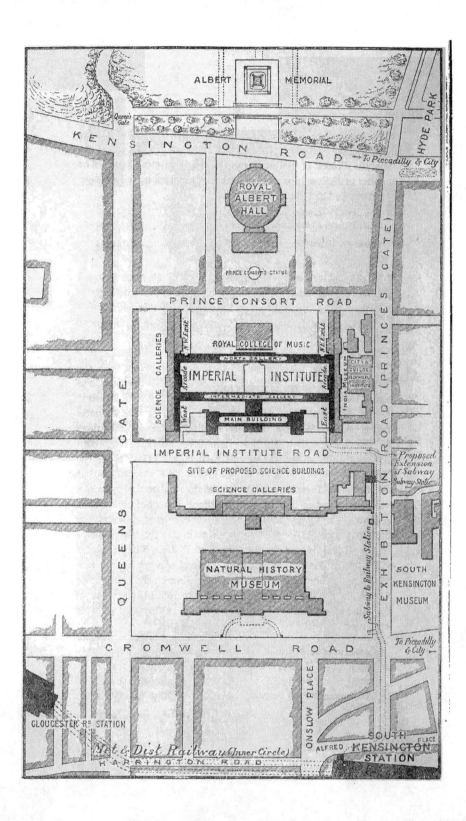

DESCRIPTION OF THE SITE AND BUILDINGS.

THE subject of a suitable site for the buildings of the Institute received early and careful consideration. The Organising Committee were fully alive to the importance of establishing the Institute in as central a position in the Metropolis as practicable, but the results of inquiries showed that there was no possibility of acquiring an adequate area of ground, either in the East Central or the West Central District, for any sum of money falling within the limits of funds likely to be received by a very general and liberal public subscription. Several sites were proffered, but in no case was the price asked much less than a quarter of a million sterling, and in no instance did the site provide an area at all approaching that required for the purposes of the Institute.

The Organising Committee, being therefore forced to abandon the hope of obtaining a central site, directed their attention to the property at South Kensington belonging to the Commissioners of the Exhibition of 1851, and a representation was submitted by the Committee to the Prince of Wales, to the effect that the Imperial Institute might reasonably advance a claim for the grant of a site of sufficient magnitude for its purposes, from the land purchased with the surplus proceeds of the first International Exhibition, which were intrusted to the Royal Commissioners of that Exhibition for application in the interests of Institutions and undertakings designed for the promotion of Science and Art. An offer was thereupon made by the Royal Commissioners of an extensive site, at a nominal rent, for the purposes of the Imperial Institute, provided that the Organising Committee would agree to the fulfilment of certain preliminary conditions; and this proposal was gladly accepted. The site cannot fail to be tolerably familiar to those who visited the series of displays commencing with the International Fisheries Exhibition in 1883, and ending with the Colonial and Indian Exhibition in 1886. The main entrance to those exhibitions in Exhibition Road, and the subsidiary entrance, together with the long connecting court devoted to India, which reached to Queen's Gate, are now supplanted by a broad avenue known as the "Imperial Institute Road," the sidewalks of which, each fifteen feet wide, will eventually be lined with trees of a like character to those on the Thames Embankment. The actual length of the building-frontage is a little over seven hundred and fifty feet, and the galleries are carried northwards to the Royal Albert Hall, the rear boundary being coincident with the southern parapet of the illuminated fountains which were overlooked by the late Prince Consort's statue. To the original donation of land have since been added the arcades which formerly enclosed the gardens of the Royal Horticultural Society, so far as they extend to the northern boundary. The new buildings of the Royal College of Music which abut upon the line of the north gallery of the Institute face the "Prince Consort Road," which is parallel with the Imperial Institute Road. Altogether the ground area of the Imperial Institute buildings and courts occupies nearly nine acres.

As soon as the site had been formally leased by the Royal Commissioners of 1851 to the Organising Committee (as the temporary Governing Body of the Imperial Institute), an outline of the general requirements, as regards buildings, was prepared and published, and several architects of high repute (Sir A. Blomfield, A.R.A., Mr. T. G. Jackson, Messrs. Webb and Ingress Bell, Mr. Rowand Anderson, Messrs. Deane and Son, and Mr. Thomas E. Collcutt) were selected to submit their plans to judges appointed by the Committee from their number (the late Earl of Carnarvon, Lord Herschell, Sir Frederick Leighton, Sir Frederick Abel, and Mr. Waterhouse, then President of the Royal Institute of British Architects). The designs sent in were all of a very high order in regard to architectural beauty and structural details; in several instances, however, their execution would have involved an outlay greatly exceeding the resources likely to be available, and the judges eventually decided to accept the designs prepared by Mr. Thomas E. Collcutt, being of opinion that these, if thoroughly carried out, would provide a monumental structure worthy to commemorate the occasion of the Institute's foundation, as well as adequate accommodation for the various functions to be fulfilled by the building, and at a cost falling within the warranted limits of expenditure.   The high honour paid to Mr. Collcutt at the Paris Exhibition in 1889, as an exhibitor of his plans of the Imperial Institute, afforded very satisfactory confirmation of the good judgment exercised by the Committee of Selection.   The erection of the main building was submitted to select competition, and, from among six firms who tendered, Messrs. Mowlem and Co., the well-known contractors, who had already been employed as constructors of the Imperial Institute Road, were entrusted with the work.

THE CENTRAL OR "QUEEN'S" TOWER.

The prevailing style of the building is a free rendering of the Renaissance, and as the amplitude of mouldings and the abundance of arabesque carvings show a decided relationship to Early Italian Renaissance, it may be said that the Imperial Institute

affords a characteristic example of the gradual movement
towards the Renaissance, as practised in this country during the
last two decades.

The crowning attraction of the foreground is the great portal,
surmounted—although set back from it—by the large square
tower, capped by a dome-shaped cupola. The altitude of this

tower is nearly three hundred feet, the two flanking towers being one hundred and seventy-six feet high. Their solidity is insured by walls nine feet thick, composed of hard bricks set in cement. Within these towers are contained tank-spaces and storerooms, and the upper chamber of the central beacon contains a complete peal of bells, ten in number, and designated, by permission of H.R.H. the Princess of Wales, as the "Alexandra" peal. The tenor is two tons in weight, and bears the following inscription: "Victoria R.I. 1837-1887"; the other bells are named after the Prince and Princess of Wales, the Duke of Edinburgh, the Duke of Connaught, and the five children of the Prince and Princess of Wales, the total weight of the ten bells being over eight tons. As placed, the peal is the highest in the country, as the bells swing in a chamber 200 feet above the level of the ground-floor of the main building. The gift was a personal one to the Prince of Wales by Mrs. E. M. Millar, of Melbourne, and the names of the various bells were approved by Her Majesty and His Royal Highness. The only condition specified by the donor was that the bells should be rung on the birthday and accession-day of the Sovereign and the birthdays of the Prince and Princess of Wales. They are to be fully completed and first rung on the occasion of the inauguration of the Institute by the Queen. The bells were cast and supplied by the well-known firm of J. Taylor and Co., of Loughborough.

Portland stone, quarried from the Whit-bed, is used in facing the front walls; this particular bed supplies a stone which combines the qualities essential for withstanding the deteriorating effects of the London atmosphere. The use of red brick enters sparingly into this portion of the work, but being confined to the recesses, it is of service in sensibly adding to the desired variations in light and shade.

The principal entrance is seventeen feet wide by twenty-three feet and a half high, and constructed altogether of Portland stone. The frieze over the arch is intended to be covered with symbolic modellings, with a central seated figure representing Her Majesty Queen Victoria. The internal screens (shown on page 13) are of richly-embellished Hopton Wood stone. This and Portland stone are associated in the vaulting. It should be said of the former that, possessing many of the characteristics of marble, it is capable of fine polish, which brings out all its delicate markings. Their pleasing effect is increased by the interposition, here and there, of Derbyshire fossil panels, extracted from the same quarries.

The Great Hall (its site is now occupied by a temporary structure of the same area) will undoubtedly, when built, be the gem of the whole fabric; it will exhibit a diversified use of various marbles and of Indian teak panelling,

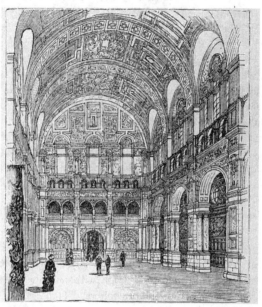

THE GREAT HALL AS IT WILL APPEAR WHEN COMPLETED.

fourteen feet high on the sides, with a richly-coffered and vaulted ceiling. Its dimensions are to be one hundred and twenty-eight feet long, by sixty feet wide; the side-aisles will be each twelve feet wide. A musicians' gallery will be provided at the southern end, and it is contemplated to raise a platform at the northern end, with all needful retiring-room accommodation.

A beautiful stairway, forming the continuation of the Vestibule.

is twenty-one feet wide, and supported by marble pilasters, arches, and other devices. From the vestibule-landing, the stairs return to the first floor by the corridors shown in the sketch. The ground-floor, on the road level, is reached from the Vestibule by flanking stairs under the main stairway. In the choice of the ornamental marbles, British (including Irish) and Colonial have prior claims ; their great expense, when com-

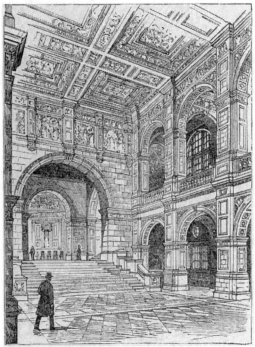

THE VESTIBULE LOOKING TOWARDS THE GREAT HALL, AS ORIGINALLY DESIGNED.*

pared with Belgian and Italian marbles, compelled, however, a limited indulgence in their employment. The ceiling is of arabesque plaster, suitably coloured.

The principal Library at the east end of the main building and the Conference Hall at the west end have to be deferred until funds for their construction have been obtained.

---

* The style of decoration has been varied from the original · design. Marble columns have taken the place of the square pillars, and oak girders support the roof.

Scarcely, if at all, inferior to the grand stairway just described is that by which access is gained, on the east side of the inner main entrance, from the principal corridor and main floor to the corridors and rooms on the first and second floors. The steps are of Hopton Wood stone, with marble balusters and rails. The ceiling is profusely decorated with arabesque plaster,

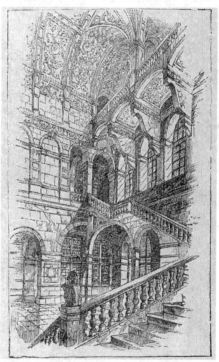

UPPER PART OF PRINCIPAL STAIRWAY TO FIRST AND SECOND FLOORS.

and has a prominent cone, forming arches to that portion leading on to the second floor. The stained-glass windows display the arms of the United Kingdom and of the different Colonies, and emblems of the Indian Empire. The mode in which the steps are upheld is worthy of notice; they are carried on marble cantilevers, and the soffits of the arches, being covered in mosaic and other ornamental material, lend themselves to colour decoration.

It is possible that a section of the interior which will command as much attention as any other is the polished stone corridor running along the entire length of the principal floor. The vaulted ceiling, elaborately panelled in arabesque work, rises twenty feet from the mosaic floor, and the passage, twelve

LOWER PART OF PRINCIPAL STAIRWAY TO FIRST AND SECOND FLOORS.

feet wide, is adequately lighted by the range of windows to the front. The arched grille, to be seen at the left of the picture is of wrought iron, the balusters below being of bronze. The doorway conducts to the post and telegraph offices, and the telephone room.

This corridor would be an excellent situation for representative

C 2

statuary. It is from it (on the west side) that the administrative
and (on the east side) Fellows' departments of the Institute are
reached. They comprise Council Room and Secretarial Offices,
four Conference Halls, dedicated to the use of groups of
Colonies, Reading and Writing Rooms, a News Room, and a
Reference Library. The first floor is in part intended for the
accommodation of organisations and societies which may eventually desire to be associated with the Institute, and comprises
rooms also adapted for small special exhibitions. A consider-

THE PRINCIPAL CORRIDOR (WEST SIDE).

able portion of its space is devoted to the Fellows' dining and
refreshment department, the kitchens of which are placed on the
top floor, as also are the smoking and billiard rooms. The
Billiard Room is fitted with full-sized tables by Messrs.
Burroughes and Watts, and Messrs. Thurston and Co. respectively. Rooms in the west corridor are allotted to the
Northbrook Society, the Anglo-Russian Literary Society (which
are affiliated to the Institute), the Map Room, the Conference
Room for the Eastern Crown Colonies, the Conference Room
for the Western Crown Colonies. The last two named are

IMPERIAL INSTITUTE

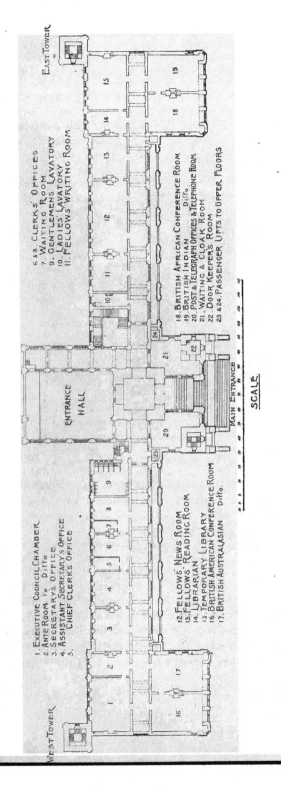

WEST TOWER

EAST TOWER

ENTRANCE HALL

MAIN ENTRANCE

SCALE

1. EXECUTIVE COUNCIL CHAMBER
2. ANTE ROOM to DITTO
3. SECRETARY'S OFFICE
4. ASSISTANT SECRETARY'S OFFICE
5. CHIEF CLERKS OFFICE

6. & 8. CLERKS' OFFICES
7. WAITING ROOM
9. GENTLEMENS LAVATORY
10. LADIES' LAVATORY
11. FELLOWS WRITING ROOM

12. FELLOWS' NEWS ROOM
13. FELLOWS' READING ROOM
14. LIBRARIAN
15. TEMPORARY LIBRARY
16. BRITISH AMERICAN CONFERENCE ROOM
17. BRITISH AUSTRALASIAN DITTO.

18. BRITISH AFRICAN CONFERENCE ROOM
19. BRITISH INDIAN DITTO
20. POST & TELEGRAPH OFFICES & TELEPHONE ROOM
21. WAITING & CLOAK ROOM
22. DOOR KEEPER'S ROOM
23. & 24. PASSENGER LIFTS TO UPPER FLOORS

PLAN OF THE PRINCIPAL FLOOR

charmingly furnished in carved oak, the walls being decorated with handsome printed velvets of appropriate design. The furniture is especially manufactured, and supplied by Messrs. R. Bowman and Co., of the Fulham Road, London. On the second or top floor will be found the public dining and

DOORWAY IN CORRIDOR OF THE PRINCIPAL FLOOR.

refreshment saloon, sample examination rooms, laboratories, and kindred apartments. The ground-floor, entered from the level of the roadway, provides ample space for stores and for classified commercial samples in bulk.

No one who is interested in artistic decoration and furnishing should omit to inspect the British American (Canadian) and the British Australasian Conference Rooms at the west end of the principal corridor. The beautiful oak panelling is a splendid specimen of English village industry, the whole of the wood having been prepared and carved in a rural parish of the county of Essex. The British Indian and the British African Conference Rooms are at the east end of the principal corridor, near the Fellows' apartments and temporary Library; they are also sumptuous chambers, the British African Room being a masterpiece of decorative art.

The Executive Council Chamber walls have been decorated most effectively by Mr. Thomas·Wardle, art printer and dyer, of Leek, Staffordshire. The material used is a coarse flax cloth upon which is printed a Spanish tapestry design, with a characteristic border in colours. The hangings are so arranged as to fall in folds, and the effect is very pleasing. The border reaches down to the top of the dado mould, thus covering the whole of

UPPER PART OF EAST AND WEST WINGS.

the walls. The Fellows' Dining and Refreshment Room Friezes have been printed in olive-green velveteen. The pattern is the "Haddon Hall" design, which was copied, by special permission of the Duke of Rutland, from the green and crimson Genoese silk velvet curtains on the state bed in Haddon Hall. It harmonises well with the oak panelling in the room. The wall hangings in the Eastern and Western Crown Colonies Conference Rooms, in the West Corridor of the First Floor, were also supplied by Mr. Wardle.

There are numerous Retiring Rooms for Ladies and Gentlemen interspersed throughout the building and grounds.

The gabled projections of the façade are fairly uniform in
style, but the increased size of those of the eastern and western
wings, by reason of their bolder outline, gave larger scope for
vigorous ornamentation. They are, of course, entirely in Portland stone.

The whole structure, with the exception of the fittings, consists
of fire-proof materials, and care has been taken to secure every
fire-proof appliance ; the building is illuminated throughout by
the electric light, and is heated in the winter season on the most
approved principles. The quadrangles at the rear, formed by
the oblong arcades, the central and north galleries, and the
temporary Great Hall, indicate the position of the ornamental
gardens, band-stands, promenades, fountains, outdoor refreshment kiosks, as well as possible areas for the future location of
special exhibitions, or for the extension of accommodation for
collections. The east end of the North-west Quadrangle, which
adjoins the East Indian Court, is occupied by the Indian Pavilion,
where a large number of very interesting objects are displayed,
and facilities provided for partaking of Indian teas and coffee.
This pavilion will adapt itself (for some months in the year) as
a very attractive winter garden.

The frontage of the main building is connected by 112-feet
colonnades* on either side, from the façades of the east and west
galleries to which reference has been made, so that the buildings
may present a continuous line along almost the entire north side
of the road. Its south side will in time be occupied by public
buildings, the Government having acquired the plot of land
facing the frontage of the Institute. It is also in contemplation to
join the convenient subway of the Metropolitan District Railway
with the eastern arcade and colonnade.

The total outlay upon the buildings and their appurtenances
as they now exist, or are in course of completion, stands at
£280,000. An addition of £80,000 to the Building Fund will be

---

* *The Eastern Colonnade, connecting the Main Building with the Indian Section,
has been erected at the expense of Mr. M. M. Bhownaggree, C.I.E., as a memorial of
his sister, Miss Awabai Merwanjee Bhownaggree.*

required before the Great Hall, the Library, and Conference Hall can be constructed ; when entirely finished, the expenditure on the Building will be represented by about £360,000.

The arrangements made by the Executive Council will provide for the exclusive use of the buildings, galleries, and commercial collections, by Fellows and business people, from 10 a.m to 3 p.m. every week-day (excepting the recognised holidays, and Good Friday and Christmas Day) throughout the year. On four days in each week, during the summer and autumn months, the general public will be admitted to the galleries and grounds, from 3.30 p.m. to 10.30 p.m., to enable all classes to take advantage of the information and entertainment that the Building and its collections and resources afford. The admission fees will be varied for different days, and be at such nominal rates as will reasonably provide for the necessary expenses involved. On Wednesdays and Fridays only Fellows and their friends (introduced with passes, of which books can be purchased by Fellows) will be admitted after 4 p.m. Instrumental music will be performed daily, in the afternoon and evening, by the best military bands.

The Regulations for, and description of the privileges of, Fellows will be found at page 51.

PLAN SHOWING PRELIMINARY AND PROVISIONAL ALLOTMENT OF SPACE

FOR DISPLAY OF PERMANENT COLLECTIONS, AND ALSO THE QUADRANGLES, VERANDAHS, PROMENADES & GARDENS.

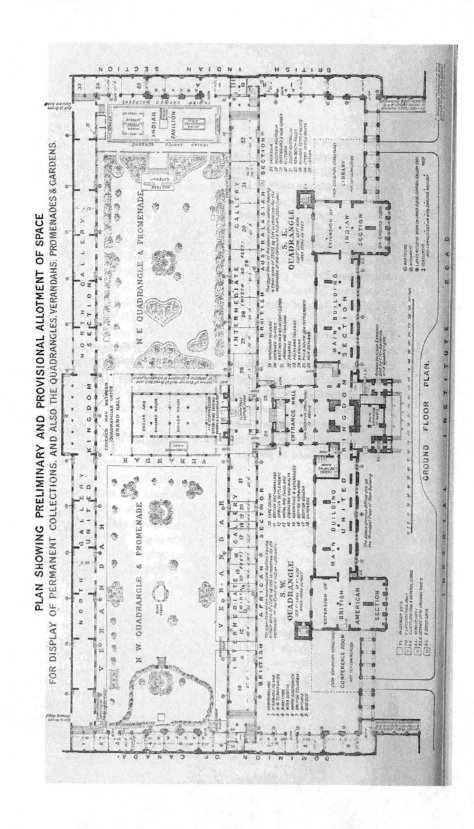

GROUND FLOOR PLAN.

THE OBJECTS AND PURPOSES OF THE IMPERIAL INSTITUTE.

THE organisation of the Institute has for its guiding principles the broad plan laid down by the Organising Committee in December 1886. The contents of the galleries will constitute a living representation of the resources of the Empire, and of the condition of its Industries and Commerce. Occasional special exhibitions of Colonial and Indian produce and of particular industries will be arranged. At one time a particular Colony or portion of the Empire may desire to show its general progress ; at another time a representation of the existing condition in the Empire of one or more particular industries may be desirable. Whilst the permanent collections will illustrate the natural and industrial products of the United Kingdom, of the several Colonies, and of India, the occasional exhibitions will, it is hoped, stimulate and enlist the sympathies of Colonial, Indian, and British producers, and promote active co-operation with the industrial section of the Empire.

The collections are being so arranged and described as to afford full scientific, practical, and commercial information relating to the sources, nature, facilities of supply, and applications of well-known natural products, and of those whose industrial or commercial value still needs development, and every effort will be made continuously to maintain them so that they shall always thoroughly illustrate existing knowledge and conditions with regard to our Imperial resources.

The Institute, through the agency of these collections, of its Libraries, Offices of Reference, Reading Rooms, and facilities for Conferences, will be a central source of information upon all matters relating to the natural and industrial resources, the trades and handicrafts, and the commerce of every part of the Empire ; it will afford facilities to all classes for acquiring practical knowledge regarding known and new materials, and information relating to inventions made and industrial achievements accomplished at home, in the Colonies, and in foreign

countries. The manufacturer, the merchant, and the tradesman
will be able to obtain through its agency samples of new
Colonial and Indian products, with particulars regarding their

ONE OF THE FOUR CONFERENCE ROOMS ALLOTTED TO BRITISH INDIA, BRITISH
AMERICA, BRITISH AUSTRALASIA, AND BRITISH AFRICA.

occurrence and history, and the Institute will, by means of Loan-
Collections and Libraries, by the organisation of Lectures and
Conferences at the Institute and at provincial centres, and by
co-operating with local commercial and trade museums, maintain
an intimate union between itself and the chief seats of commerce
and industry throughout the United Kingdom.

The charter, by which the Organising Committee was made
the temporary governing body, sets out in considerable detail
the purposes and objects of the Institute, as follows :—

1. The formation and exhibition of collections representing the important raw
materials and manufactured products of the Empire and of other countries, so maintained as to illustrate the development of agricultural, commercial, and industrial
progress in the Empire, and the comparative advances made in other countries.

2. The establishment or promotion of commercial museums, sample-rooms, and intelligence offices, in London and other parts of the Empire.

3. The collection and dissemination of such information relating to trades and industries, to emigration, and to the other purposes of the charter as may be of use to the subjects of the Empire.

4. The advancement of trades and handicrafts by exhibitions of special branches of industry and commerce, and of the work of artisans and of apprentices.

5. The promotion of technical and commercial education, and of the industrial arts and sciences.

6. The furtherance of systematic colonisation.

7. The promotion of conferences and lectures in connection with the general work of the Institute, and the facilitating of commercial and friendly intercourse among the inhabitants of the different parts of the British Empire.

8. The doing anything incidental or conducive to carrying into effect all or any of the foregoing purposes.

The hearty co-operation and important material support which the great Colonies have already given, and have pledged themselves to in the future, afford conclusive evidence of their earnest desire to be in all respects thoroughly represented in the Mother Country, and to take their places side by side with the representatives of commerce and industries in the United Kingdom as fellow-labourers in the advancement of the prosperity of the Empire. In furtherance of this important end, a notable feature of the building will be the attractions and conveniences presented by it as a place of resort, a club, and a *rendezvous* for Colonists visiting England, and, it is also anticipated, for members of the important Societies which represent the Colonies and the Asiatic possessions in this country. A commencement has been made in this direction by the affiliation to the Institute of the Northbrook Society, which now has its home in the building. The Institute will afford ample facilities for reference to literature concerning the Colonies and India, for conferences on matters of common interest and value to the Colonists and those at home, for the interchange of information between the British manufacturer and those in the Colonies who are directly interested in meeting his requirements, and, generally, for the cultivation of intimate relations and good fellowship between ourselves and our brethren from all parts of the Empire. It will, however, not simply operate actively under its own roof in promoting the cultivation of a better knowledge of the geography, natural history, and resources of our Colonies, and for the advancement of the interests of the Colonists in this country ; for it is contemplated that representative collections of the natural products of the Colonies and India, carefully identified with the more elaborate collections in the Institute itself, shall be distributed to provincial centres, and that the provinces shall be kept thoroughly conversant with the current information from the Colonies and India, bearing upon the interests of the commercial man, the manufacturer, and the intending emigrant.

The Colonies and the Indian Empire cannot fail to be greatly benefited by being thoroughly represented in a well-selected and carefully-organised assemblage of illustrations of the sources of prosperity which constitute the sinews of their commerce, the continuous exploration and cultivation of which are vital to the maintenance of the influence of each section of the Empire upon industrial and social progress. Neither can the denizens of all parts of the Empire fail to reap substantial advantages by pursuing a friendly rivalry with each other in demonstrating the advances made from time to time in the development of the resources of the respective countries in which their lot is cast.

Without taking any direct part in the duty of education, it is contemplated that the Imperial Institute will, in due course, actively assist in the thorough organisation of technical instruction at home and in the Colonies, and in its maintenance on a footing, at least of equality, with that provided in other countries. Efforts will be made to establish and maintain a system of intercommunication between technical and science schools, by the distribution of information relating to the progress of technical education abroad, the progressive development of industries, and the requirements of those who intend to pursue them ; by the provision of resources in the way of material for experimental work, of illustrations of new industrial achievements, and by the furtherance of any measure tending to promote industrial progress. The provision of facilities to teachers in elementary schools to improve their knowledge of science and their power of imparting information of an elementary character to the young, with the aid of simple practical demonstrations of scientific principles involved in the proceedings of daily life, constitutes another direction in which it is hoped that the operations of the Institute may promote progress towards the establishment of that continuity between elementary and advanced education which is so well developed on the continent of Europe.

By the establishment of an educational Enquiry Branch of the Intelligence Department, which is already a prominent section of the Imperial Institute, the working of the colleges and schools of applied science; in all parts of the United Kingdom may be assisted, and information continuously collected from all countries relating to educational work may be systematically distributed. Measures will be adopted for enabling the Enquiry Department to furnish to students coming to Great Britain from the Colonies, Dependencies, and India the requisite information and advice to aid them in selecting their place of work and their temporary home, and in various other ways. The collections of natural products of the Colonies and India, maintained up to the day, by additions and renewals, at the central establishment of the Institute, will be of great value to students in the immediately adjacent educational Institutions, and will moreover be made subservient to the purposes of provincial industrial colleges by the distribution of thoroughly descriptive reference-catalogues, and of specimens. Supplies of natural products from the Colonies, India, or from other countries, which are either new or have been but imperfectly studied, will be maintained, so that material may be readily provided to the worker in science or the manufacturer, either for scientific investigation or for purposes of technical experiment and commercial utilisation.

The existence of those collections and of all information relating to them, as well as of a library of technology, inventions, commerce and applied geography, and a well-equipped map room, in immediate proximity to the Government Museums of Science and Inventions, Art, and Natural History, to the Normal School of Science, and to the Central Technical Institute, presents advantages so obvious as to have merited fair consideration by those who at the outset declined to recognise any reason in favour of the establishment of the Imperial Institute on its present site.

In the powerful public representations which have of late been made on the imperative necessity for a wider dissemination and thorough organisation of industrial education, the importance of a radical improvement in commercial education, as distinguished from what is comprehended under the head of technical training, has received prominent notice. It is within the scope of the Imperial Institute, as an organisation for the advancement of industry and commerce, to promote a systematic improvement and organisation of commercial education by measures analogous to those which it will bring to bear upon the advancement of industrial education.

Measures have already been carried out for organising and extending the facilities in the Metropolis for the study of Modern Oriental Languages, the nature of which is explained at page 25.

Of the special functions to be fulfilled by the Institute, none will be more important than those most immediately connected alike with the great commercial work of the City of London and with that of the provincial centres of commerce. The provision, in very central and readily accessible positions, of commercial museums or collections of natural or import products, and of export products of different nations, combined with comprehensive sample-rooms and facilities for the business of inspection or of commercial, chemical or physical examination, is a work in which the Institute may lend most important aid. The system of correspondence with all parts of the Empire which it will organise and maintain will enable it to form a central depôt of natural products from which local commercial museums can be supplied with complete, thoroughly classified economic collections, and with representative samples of all that, from time to time, is new in the way of natural products from the Colonies and Dependencies, from India, and from other countries. In combination with this organisation, the distribution, to commercial centres, of information acquired by a central department of commercial geography will constitute an important feature in the work of the Institute, bearing immediately upon the interests of the merchant at home, in the Colonies, and in India.

The gradual establishment in this way, through the agency of the Institute in different parts of the Empire, of specially commercial institutions, of which enquiry offices, museums, and sample-rooms with their accessories, form leading features, will supply a want long since provided for by some of the nations with whom we compete commercially, and our great commercial centres will doubtless speedily take steps to provide accommodation for such offshoots from the central collections of the Institute.

The well-tried machinery of the War Office Intelligence Department has served as a guide for the elaboration of a Commercial Intelligence Department. This Department, which has commenced its operations by establishing relations with the chief Colonies and India, will be in constant communication with the Enquiry Offices to be attached to the local commercial establishments and to other provincial representations of the work of the Institute, and will systematically distribute among them the commercial information and statistics continuously collected. It will be equally valuable to the Colonies and to India by bringing their requirements thoroughly to the knowledge of business men in the United Kingdom, and by maintaining that close touch and sympathy between the Colonists, amongst themselves, and with the people at home, which will tend to a true federation of all parts of the Empire.

The first outcome of the work of the Intelligence Department has already appeared in the form of a very comprehensive and thoroughly authoritative Year-Book. The several sections of this work are periodically submitted to the Governments of the Colonies concerned, and, in all instances, receive careful official revision.

The general details of the work of the Institute are directed by seven standing Committees, acting under the supervision and approval of the Executive Council. There are, in addition many sub-Committees, who deal with specific subjects and references. The Governing Body exercises its powers through the medium of the Executive Council and these Committees, respecting which full particulars are given at pages 64-68.

D

IMPERIAL INSTITUTE

WEST TOWER

EAST TOWER

UPPER PART OF ENTRANCE HALL

FELLOWS DINING ROOM

1, 2, 6, 12, 13, MEETING ROOMS FOR SOCIETIES
3, WESTERN CROWN COLONIES CONFERENCE ROOM
4, EASTERN   Ditto
5, NORTHBROOK SOCIETY'S ROOM

7, GENTLEMENS' LAVATORY
8, 9, 10, 11, COMMERCIAL INTELLIGENCE DEPTS
1, MAP ROOM
15, 16, 17, COMMERCIAL CONFERENCE ROOMS
18 & 19, PASSENGER LIFTS

PLAN OF FIRST FLOOR

RULES AND REGULATIONS WITH RESPECT TO FELLOWS AND THE PRIVILEGES ATTACHING TO FELLOWSHIP.

ELECTION, SUBSCRIPTIONS, AND PRIVILEGES OF FELLOWS.

I.—As to Privileges of Fellows.

Every Fellow elected in the manner provided by the Regulations approved under the Charter of Incorporation shall during the continuance of his Fellowship be entitled to attach to his name the distinctive designation " F. I. Inst."

Every Fellow, upon his election, shall receive a diploma, or other emblem of his Fellowship.

Fellows shall be entitled to the Annual Report of the Institute, and to Publications issued from time to time by the Institute, subject to such arrangements as may be made by the Executive Council as to the delivery or transmission of the same.

Fellows shall have access to the Commercial and Industrial Collections on two days in the week when they are *not* open to the public, and shall on any one of those days have the privilege of introducing two visitors to the Collections.

A special Refreshment Department, including Smoking Room, will be provided for the use of Fellows, to which they will be entitled, on any day, to introduce two visitors.

The accommodation provided for the use of Fellows will include a Post Office and *Poste Restante*, Telegraph-, Telephone-, and Messenger Departments, Cloak Room and Parcels Office, and Private Lavatory.

Fellows will have the free use of the Library, the News Room and Reference Department connected therewith, the Map Room, Reading Rooms, Writing Room and Conference Rooms, and shall be entitled to introduce one visitor on any day to those rooms. The Conference Rooms will include special

Rooms for the use of Fellows and visitors from the Australasian,. the North American and the African Colonies, from India, and from the Crown Colonies. Facilities will be afforded to Fellows, at moderate charges, for holding business Conferences at the Institute, involving the exclusive occupation of a room for specified periods, with or without clerical assistance.

Fellows will be entitled to admission to special conferences, addresses, discussions, or lectures, under regulations to be determined upon by the Council, and will have the privilege of introducing visitors, in conformity with those regulations.

The Commercial Intelligence or Information Department will be open to Fellows between the hours of 10 a.m. and 1 p.m.,. and 2 p.m. and 4 p.m. on Mondays to Fridays inclusive; and between 10 a.m. and noon on Saturdays.

Facilities will be afforded to Fellows to inspect or to specially examine, or to be supplied with, samples of materials and products included in the collections, under regulations and Conditions to be determined by the Council, and, if necessary, upon payment of such fees as will compensate the Institute for any loss or special outlay connected with such inspection, for which special localities and appliances will be provided.

II.—As to Proposal and Election of Fellows.

(*Abstract of Regulations.*)

A Candidate for admission as an Ordinary Fellow must be proposed and seconded by two Fellows from personal knowledge; such proposal, which shall specify the rank, profession or occupation, and place of abode of the Candidate, must, in addition, be signed by two Fellows at least.

The certificate of proposal thus filled up, as soon as it has been delivered to the Secretary, shall be exhibited in a conspicuous place in one or other of the public rooms of the Institute for at least one week previous to the date of election.

Candidates proposed as Fellows shall, from time to time, be submitted for election at a meeting of the Executive Council, in accordance with the prescribed Regulations.

III.—As to Subscriptions to be Paid by Fellows.

(Abstract of Regulations.)

The annual subscription to the Institute shall, subject to the provisions contained in the regulations next following, be *Two Pounds*. From and after such date as may be appointed by the Executive Council, an Entrance Fee may be imposed.

Any Fellow who intends to be absent from the United Kingdom during the whole time for which the Annual Subscription is payable, shall, on his giving due notice in writing to the Secretary of such intention, pay an Annual Subscription of *One Pound* only, during the continuance of such absence. If such Fellow returns to the United Kingdom, he may, on communicating the fact in writing to the Secretary, and on paying such sum as may be required to make up his subscription for the current year to the full amount of *Two Pounds*, be re-admitted to all the privileges of the Institute.

Any Fellow who, at the time of his election, is resident out of the United Kingdom, shall pay an Annual Subscription of *One Pound* only, during the continuance of such residence. If such Fellow comes to the United Kingdom, he may, on communicating the fact in writing to the Secretary, avail himself, for a period not exceeding three months from the date of his arrival, of all the privileges of the Institute. If he resides within the United Kingdom beyond that period he will be required to make up his subscription for the current year to the full amount of *Two Pounds*.

A newly-elected Fellow shall not be entitled to exercise any of the privileges of a Fellow until he has paid his first year's subscription, or entrance fee and first year's subscription, as the case may be, or has compounded as hereinafter provided.

All subscriptions, after the subscription due at election, shall be payable on the 1st January in each year.

When a Candidate becomes a Fellow late in the year the Executive Council may remit the whole or such part as they may think just of his subscription for the current year.

Any Fellow may compound for his subscription and become a life Fellow, either at his entrance by the payment of *Twenty Pounds*, or, after the payment of five or more annual subscriptions, by the payment of *Fifteen Pounds*.

NOTE.—*In conformity with Clause 67 of the Constitution approved by Royal Warrant, the Executive Council may, from time to time, repeal, alter or add to these Rules respecting the Election, Subscriptions and Privileges of Fellows.*

The Executive Council at its meeting on the 15th of July, 1892, and under the powers of the Constitution, adopted the following Regulations, in addition to the above :—

The Wives of Fellows shall be admitted to all the privileges of Fellowship of the Imperial Institute on election and payment of an Annual Subscription of One Pound.

The Executive Council reserves the right to restrict the admittance of Fellows to particular apartments on a fixed number of days during the year, of the number of which notice will shortly be given.

The Executive Council at its meeting on the 24th January, 1893, under the same powers, further adopted the following Resolution :—

Any Fellow who at the time of his election is resident out of the United Kingdom may, with the stipulation given below, compound for his subscription and become a Life Fellow by payment at his entrance of *Ten Pounds*. If such Fellow comes to the United Kingdom he may, after communicating the fact in writing to the Secretary, avail himself, for a period not exceeding three months from the date of his arrival, of all the privileges of the Institute ; but should he reside within the United Kingdom beyond that period, he cannot continue to enjoy the

privileges of a Home Member unless he pay a subscription of *One Pound* for the current year, and for any
succeeding year during which he may remain in the
United Kingdom.

A detachable Form of Application for Fellowship will be
found on page 59.

PROVISIONAL REGULATIONS FOR THE USE OF THE
BUILDINGS, GALLERIES, AND GROUNDS BY FELLOWS
DURING THE SUMMER AND AUTUMN SEASON, ON AND
FROM THURSDAY, MAY 18TH, 1893.

*The Executive Council have adopted the following Regulations,
which are subject to amendment and alteration from time to time
as may be expedient :—*

PRIVILEGES EXCLUSIVELY RESERVED TO FELLOWS.

On and after Thursday, May 18th, 1893, the undermentioned
Apartments and Portions of the Building will be open to
Fellows, and to Friends personally introduced by them in
accordance with the Regulations now in force, every week-day
from 10 a.m. to 11.30 p.m., and on Sundays from 3 p.m. to
10.30 p.m. :—

The Library,
The News Room,
The Writing Room,   } One Friend on any day.
The Reading Room,
The Map Room.

The Fellows' Luncheon and
    Dining Room,
The Fellows' Smoking   } Two Friends on any day.
    Room, and
The Fellows' Billiard Room.

From 10 a.m. to 3 p.m. on Wednesdays and Fridays (Public

Holidays excepted), the following portions of the Building will be open for the inspection and use of Fellows and Friends :—

The Collections,
The Indian Pavilion,
The Commercial Intelligence Department, and
The Sample Stores.

} Two Friends on any day.

The Gardens will be exclusively reserved for the use of Fellows and their Friends on Wednesdays and Fridays.

After 3 p.m. on Wednesdays and Fridays the above portions of the buildings and the gardens will be exclusively reserved for the use of Fellows, and of Friends introduced by them, with Tickets which must bear a Fellow's signature. These tickets will be procurable by Fellows only at the Ticket Office of the Institute, on payment of One Guinea for each book of fifteen Tickets. Money will not be taken at any of the entrances on Wednesdays and Fridays. Fellows must show their Fellowship Cards or Passes on every occasion at the gates and doors specially reserved for them. The Galleries and Grounds will be cleared at 11 p.m. on Wednesdays and Fridays.

The Main Entrance will be at all times reserved for Fellows and Friends accompanying them.

Fellows must enter the names of Friends (not exceeding two) introduced by them into the Fellows' Luncheon and Dining Room, in the Book kept by the Doorkeeper for that purpose. [This restriction does not apply to the Public Dining Room.] Applications for reserved tables should be addressed to the Dining Room Superintendent early in the day.

Entertainments of Vocal and Instrumental Music will occasionally be given in the Great Hall and the Indian Pavilion.

Military and other Bands will play in the Kiosk of the West Garden from 3.30 to 5.30 p.m., and 8.30 to 10.30 p.m.

Retiring Rooms are reserved for Fellows on the Principal Floor : For Gentlemen, opposite the " Lift," and for Ladies between the entrance to the West Corridor of the Principal Floor and the Fellows' Writing Room.

Smoking will be permitted only in the Fellows' Smoking Room, the Billiard Room, and the Gardens.

ARRANGEMENTS FOR BUSINESS PEOPLE OTHER THAN FELLOWS.

Fellows may introduce Representatives of Commerce and Industries, for business purposes only, during the same hours as are available for Fellows (10 a.m. to 3 p.m.), to the following portions of the Building, on signing their names and description in the books kept for that purpose in the Enquiry Office.

The Public News Room,	The Map Room,
The Collections of Products,	The Sample Stores, and
The Commercial Intelligence Department,	The Public Luncheon and Dining Room.

The arrangements for the General Public will be notified hereafter.

IMPERIAL INSTITUTE

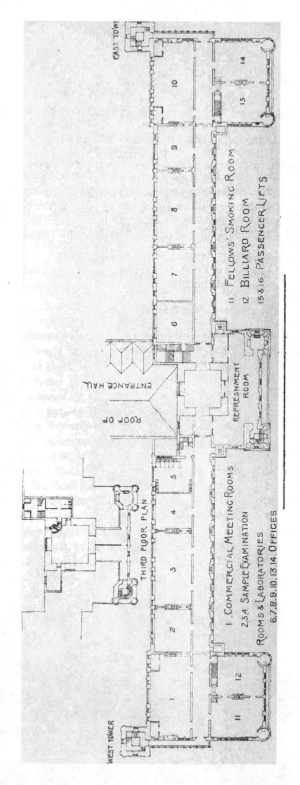

PLAN OF SECOND FLOOR

WEST TOWER

THIRD FLOOR PLAN

ROOF OF

ENTRANCE HALL

REFRESHMENT ROOM

EAST TOWER

1. COMMERCIAL MEETING ROOMS
2,3,4. SAMPLE EXAMINATION ROOMS & LABORATORIES
6.7.8.9.10.13.14. OFFICES

11 FELLOWS' SMOKING ROOM
12 BILLIARD ROOM
15 & 16 PASSENGER LIFTS

IMPERIAL INSTITUTE.

FORM OF CANDIDATE'S CERTIFICATE.

CERTIFICATE OF CANDIDATE FOR ELECTION.

* *Name*_____

† *Description*_____

*Residence*_____

_____

being desirous of admission into the Imperial Institute,

We, the undersigned, recommend h____ as likely to become a useful and valuable Fellow and Member.

*Dated this*____*day of*____, 18____.

_____ *F. I. Inst.* { *From personal knowledge.*

_____ *F. I. Inst.*

*Proposed*____, 18____.

*Elected*____, 18____.

☞ By Clause 66 of the Constitution it is declared that " Women shall be entitled. to become Members of the Institute."

---

* Please give names in full.

† Please give full list of titles or designations, particularly specifying if " Mr.," " " Mrs.," or " Miss."

This Form may be detached, filled up, and forwarded to the Secretary of The Imperial Institute, London, S.W.

GENERAL INFORMATION.

THE Imperial Institute occupies a central position between the Natural History (British) Museum, the South Kensington Museum, the Royal College of Science, the City and Guilds of London Technical Institute, the Royal College of Music, and the Royal Albert Hall. It is within five minutes' walk of Kensington Gardens, Hyde Park, and the South Kensington and Gloucester Road Stations of the Metropolitan and District Railways. There is a subway from South Kensington Station to a point close to the south corner of the Imperial Institute Road, that is to say, within about 100 yards of the main entrance, and less than that from the subsidiary entrance by the east arcade. Trains run about every ten minutes from eight o'clock in the morning until midnight to and from the following stations :—

> South Kensington (for Exhibition Road and east end of the Imperial Institute).
> Sloane Square (for Knightsbridge, &c.).
> Victoria (London and Brighton, and London Chatham and Dover Railways).
> St. James' Park (for upper end of Victoria Street, &c.).
> Westminster Bridge (for Houses of Parliament, &c.).
> Charing Cross (West Central District, and South Eastern and London and South Western Railways).
> Temple (for the Law Courts).
> Blackfriars (for Fleet Street, Ludgate Hill, &c.).
> Mansion House (for East Central District, and Royal Exchange, Bank of England, &c.).
> Cannon Street (East Central District).
> Monument (for London Bridge, Custom House, &c.).

Mark Lane (for Corn Exchange, &c.).

Aldgate (east end of City, and London and Tilbury Railway).

Bishopsgate (for Great Eastern and North London Railways).

Moorgate Street (for Wool Exchange, &c.).

Aldersgate Street (for General Post Office, &c.).

Farringdon Street (for Central Meat Market, &c.).

King's Cross (for Great Northern and Midland Railways).

Gower Street (for London and North Western Railway).

Portland Road (for Regent's Park and neighbourhood).

Baker Street (for Regent's Park and neighbourhood).

Edgware Road (Hyde Park and neighbourhood).

Praed Street (for Great Western Railway).

Queen's Road (for Bayswater and neighbourhood).

Notting Hill Gate (for West Kensington, &c.).

High Street (for Kensington).

Gloucester Road (for Queen's Gate and west end of the Institute).

From the Mansion House Station there are subsidiary services which provide trains to South Kensington and Gloucester Road nearly every three minutes throughout the day. The time occupied in reaching the Institute buildings by railway is—

From Mark Lane	28 minutes.
„ Monument	26 „
„ Cannon Street	24 „
„ Mansion House	22 „
„ Charing Cross	14 „
„ Victoria	7 „
„ Bishopsgate	37 „
„ King's Cross	28 „
„ Praed Street	15 „

Omnibuses ply every few minutes throughout the day from Liverpool Street Station and other central points in the City. One line, by the Strand, Piccadilly and Knightsbridge, enables passengers to alight at the north end of Exhibition Road

(Prince's Gate) and Queen's Gate, in close proximity to the Institute. The other line of omnibuses pursues the same route through Knightsbridge, but turns off at Brompton Road and Thurlow Place, close to the South Kensington Station, within five minutes' walk of the Institute. It is contemplated that an omnibus service to traverse the Imperial Institute Road will be shortly established.

The following are the legal cab fares from various points in the Metropolis to the Imperial Institute :—

		s.	d.
Liverpool Street Station	.. ..	2	6
Cannon Street ,,	.. ..	2	6
Charing Cross ,.	.. ..	1	6
Euston ,,	.. ..	2	0
Fenchurch Street ,,	.. ..	2	6
King's Cross ,,	.. ..	2	0
St. Pancras ,,	.. ..	2	0
London Bridge ,,	.. ..	2	6
Holborn Viaduct ,,	.. ..	2	0
Moorgate Street ,,	.. ..	2	6
Paddington ,,	.. ..	1	6
Victoria ,,	.. ..	1	0
Waterloo ,,	.. ..	2	0

The Institute is connected with the National Telephone Company of the Metropolis, the "calling" number being 8743.

The Institute is provided with a Post Office, a Poste Restante, and Telegraph and Messenger Services. Telegraphic instruments and recorders have also been provided.

The contractors for the Dining and Refreshment Rooms throughout the buildings are the firm of J. Lyons & Co., Limited, of Olympia.

STANDING COMMITTEES.

FINANCE COMMITTEE.

LORD HERSCHELL, Chairman (*ex officio*).

Mr. G. G. Arbuthnot.
Sir Daniel Cooper.
Mr. C. Washington Eves.
Mr. A. W. Gadesden.
Governor of the Bank of England.

Rt. Hon. W. Lidderdale.
Sir A. Rollit.
Lord Rothschild.
Mr. J. Watney.
Sir Alexander Wilson.

COMMITTEE OF SELECTION.

LORD HERSCHELL, Chairman (*ex officio*).

Professor Ayrton.
Sir B. C. Brown.
Lord Carrington.
Mr. E. Harford.
Alderman Horgan.
Sir W. W. Hunter.
Marquis of Lorne.
Marquis of Lothian.

Sir J. Muir, of Deanston.
Mr. J. Musgrave.
Viscount Oxenbridge.
Mr. Stuart Rendel.
Sir Saul Samuel.
Viscount Stormont.
Lord Thring.

THE COMMITTEE OF COMMERCE AND INDUSTRIES.

LORD HERSCHELL, Chairman (*ex officio*).

H.R.H. the Duke of York, K.G.
Dr. William Anderson.
Mr. H. C. Beeton.
Sir Lowthian Bell.
Sir B. C. Browne.
The President of the Associated Chambers of Commerce (Sir Albert Rollit).
Mr. A. M. Chambers.
Mr. E. Rider Cook.
Sir A. W. Croft.
The Lord Mayor of Dublin.
The Lord Provost of Edinburgh.
Mr. F. Elkington.
Mr. J. J. Fellows.
The Earl of Feversham.

Mr. Harrison Hayter.
Mr. Angus Holden.
Sir William Houldsworth.
Dr. John Kells Ingram.
Mr. H. J. Jourdain.
Sir James Kitson.
The Rt. Hon. W. Lidderdale.
The Lord Mayor of London.
Mr. Michael Murphy.
Sir Rawson W. Rawson.
The President of the Royal Statistical Society.
Sir Henry Tyler.
Sir Henry Hussey Vivian.
Mr. John Wilson.
Alderman J. Woodhouse.

COMMITTEE FOR THE COLONIES.

LORD HERSCHELL, Chairman (*ex officio*).

The Earl of Aberdeen.	Sir James Garrick.
Mr. H. C. Beeton.	Sir A. H. Gordon.
Sir G. F. Bowen.	Sir W. Drummond Jervois.
Sir E. N. Braddon.	The Marquis of Lorne.
Sir John Cox Bray.	Sir Charles Mills.
Sir W. Buller.	Mr. Westby B. Perceval.
Lord Carrington.	Mr. Peter Redpath.
Sir Andrew Clarke (*temporary*).	Sir Hercules Robinson.
Sir Daniel Cooper.	Sir Saul Samuel.
Mr. W. Dunn.	Sir Lintorn Simmons.
Mr. C. Washington Eves.	Mr. H. Spensley.
Sir Malcolm Fraser.	Sir Charles Tupper.
Sir Sanford Freeling.	Mr. Austin R. Whiteway.

COMMITTEE FOR INDIA.

LORD HERSCHELL, Chairman (*ex officio*).

Sir F. F. Adam.	The Duke of Fife.
Mr. G. G. Arbuthnot.	Mr. W. S. Halsey.
Mr. B. H. Baden-Powell.	Sir W. W. Hunter.
Colonel C. Bowen.	Mr. John Muir, of Deanston.
Mr. J. A. Bryce.	Mr. Dadabhai Naoroji.
Sir O. T. Burne.	Sir John Strachey.
Mr. D. F. Carmichael.	General J. T. Walker.
Ceylon, the Representative of.	Dr. Watt.
Sir M. S. Grant Duff.	Sir R. West.
Mr. W. T. Thiselton Dyer.	Sir A. Wilson.

COMMITTEE OF COLONIZATION AND EMIGRATION.

LORD HERSCHELL, Chairman (*ex officio*).

Associated Chambers of Commerce, Vice-Pres. of (Mr. J. F. Firth).	Mr. E. Harford.
	Sir Wm. Houldsworth.
Mr. H. C. Beeton.	Sir T. McIlwraith.
Sir G. F. Bowen.	Mr. J. Musgrave.
Mr. W. Dunn.	Sir Hercules Robinson.
Sir Sanford Freeling.	Sir Hussey Vivian.
Sir James Garrick.	Mr. A. R. Whiteway.

E

COMMITTEE FOR PUBLICATIONS AND LIBRARY,

LORD HERSCHELL, Chairman (*ex officio*).

Professor Ayrton.
Sir Lowthian Bell.
Sir E. N. Braddon.
Sir O. T. Burne.
The Earl of Ducie.
Sir M. Grant Duff.
The Duke of Fife.
Sir A. H. Gordon
Rt. Hon. J. T. Hibbert.
Mr. R. D. M. Littler.

Sir D. Maclagan.
Dr. John Rae.
Viscount Powerscourt.
Royal Institute of British Architects,
President of (Mr. J. M. Anderson).
Sir J. L. Simmons.
Mr. H. B. T. Strangways.
Sir R. West.
Admiral Sir G. Willes.

SPECIAL COMMITTEES.

SPECIAL BUILDINGS AND HOUSE COMMITTEE.

LORD HERSCHELL, Chairman (*ex officio*).

Dr. Anderson.
*Mr. J. Wolfe Barry.
*Sir Frederick Bramwell.
Prof. H. E. Armstrong.
Mr. C. Washington Eves.
Mr. A. W. Gadesden.
Sir Frederick Leighton.

*Mr. Charles Lucas.
Mr. W. H. Preece.
Royal Institute of British Architects,
    President of (Mr. J. M. Anderson).
Mr. Peter Redpath.
*Mr. A. Waterhouse.

SPECIAL COMMITTEE FOR INDIAN COLLECTIONS.

LORD HERSCHELL, Chairman (*ex officio*).

*Sir George Birdwood.
Colonel C. Bowen.
Mr. J. A. Bryce.
Sir W. W. Hunter.

General J. T. Walker.
Dr. Watt.
Sir Alexander Wilson.

With power to add three to their body.

SPECIAL COMMITTEE FOR COLONIAL COLLECTIONS.

LORD HERSCHELL, Chairman (*ex officio*).

*LORD BRASSEY, Vice-Chairman.

H.R.H. THE DUKE OF YORK, K.G.

*Sir Augustus Adderley.
Mr. H. C. Beeton.
Sir E. Braddon.
Sir John Bray.
Mr. C. Washington Eves.

Sir Charles Mills.
*Sir Montagu Ommanney.
Mr. W. B. Perceval.
Mr. Peter Redpath.

With power to add three to their body.

---

* Specially selected (not Members of the Governing Body).

SPECIAL COMMITTEE FOR PUBLICATIONS AND LIBRARY.

*Mr. C. Atchley.
Professor Ayrton.
Sir E. Braddon.
Sir A. H. Gordon.

*Mr. R. Rost.
*Mr. H. R. Tedder.
*Mr. E. Maunde Thompson.
Sir R. West.

SPECIAL COMMITTEE FOR THE MANAGEMENT OF THE SCHOOL OF MODERN ORIENTAL STUDIES.

Established by the Imperial Institute in union with University and King's Colleges, London.

LORD HERSCHELL, Chairman (*ex officio*).

*Sir Frederick Abel.
*Prof. T. W. Rhys Davids.
*Prof. R. K. Douglas.
*Sir Frederic Goldsmid.
*Sir Philip Magnus.
*Prof. Max Müller.

*The Rev. Henry Wace.
*Sir Thomas Wade.
*Lieut-Col. C. M. Watson.
*Sir Charles Wilson.
*Sir George Young.

* Specially selected (not Members of the Governing Body).

LONDON: PRINTED BY WILLIAM CLOWES AND SONS, LIMITED, STAMFORD STREET AND CHARING CROSS.

Apollinaris

"THE QUEEN OF TABLE WATERS."

"AN ABSOLUTELY PURE and AGREEABLE TABLE WATER available in every part of the World."

"REIGNS ALONE AMONG NATURAL DIETETIC TABLE WATERS."

"ITS NUMEROUS COMPETITORS APPEAR TO HAVE ONE AFTER ANOTHER FALLEN AWAY." British Medical Journal.

" More wholesome than any Aërated Water which art can supply." The TIMES.

"The LEADING DIETETIC TABLE WATER." New York Tribune.

Of all Chemists, Grocers, Wine Merchants, and Mineral Water Dealers.

All Communications respecting Advertisements for the Publications of the Imperial Institute, should be addressed to Mr. JOHN HART, Maltravers House, Arundel Street, Strand, W.C.

E. BROWN & SON'S

Boot Preparations

FOR

ORDINARY LEATHER,
PATENT LEATHER,
GLACÉ KID,

AND

BROWN LEATHER

(Light or Dark).

SOLD
EVERYWHERE.

MELTONIAN BLACKING.	MELTONIAN CREAM.	ROYAL LUTETIAN CREAM.	NONPAREIL DE GUICHE. PARISIAN POLISH.
(As used in the Royal Household) renders the Boots Soft, Durable, and Waterproof.	(WHITE OR BLACK.) Cannot be equalled for Renovating all kinds of Glacé Kid Boots and Shoes.	The best for cleaning and Polishing Russian and Brown Leather Boots, Tennis Shoes, &c.	(For Varnishing Dress Boots and Shoes) is more elastic and easier to use than any other.

7, GARRICK STREET, LONDON, W.C.,

AND 26, RUE BERGÈRE, PARIS.

ONLY COUNCIL MEDAL, LONDON, 1851.

Established in Paris, 1780.

Licensed by
King Louis XVI., 1785.

Established in London, 1792.

Gold Medals, Paris, 1819,
1823, 1827, 1834, 1844, 1851, 1878, etc.

Two Medals, Sydney, 1879.

Three Medals, Melbourne, 1880.

Gold Medal, Kimberley, 1892.

GRAND PRIX, PARIS, 1889.

Pianoforte and Harp Makers
to
Her Majesty Queen Victoria.

T.R.H. The Prince and
Princess of Wales.

H.M. The Queen of Spain.

H.M. The Queen of
the Belgians, etc.

THE ERARD
GOLD MEDAL
PIANOS· AND HARPS
ARE ABSOLUTELY WITHOUT RIVAL.

S. & P. ERARD,
MAKERS TO H.I.M. THE QUEEN AND THE ROYAL FAMILY.
18 Great Marlborough Street, London, W.

"No better Food exists."—*London Medical Record.*
This Food should be tried wherever other nourishment has not proved entirely satisfactory. It is already Cooked—requires neither boiling nor straining—is made in a minute.

Allen & Hanburys'
Infants' Food.

A Nutriment peculiarly adapted to the digestive organs of Infants and Young Children, supplying all that is required for the formation of firm flesh and bone. Surprisingly beneficial results have attended the use of this Food, and it needs only to be tried to be permanently adopted.

The **BRITISH MEDICAL JOURNAL** writes:—

"We have taken some trouble to have this food carefully tested by skilled persons, the result being decidedly satisfactory. Delicate children have in many instances, improved under its use; infants who have thriven under its use fell off when it was discontinued, and it was generally liked by the children to whom it was given. In two large *crèches* the Food has been found very successful; in more than one instance the children who have been subject to sickness being freed from it by the use of Messrs. ALLEN & HANBURYS' food. The food may be prepared either for infants or for invalids, according to the directions given; and we have no doubt whatever that this Malted Farinaceous Food will be found very effective, digestible, nutritious, and palatable wherever it be tried."

"My child after being at Death's door for weeks from exhaustion, consequent on severe diarrhœa, and inability to retain any form of 'Infants' Food' or Milk, began to improve immediately he took your malted preparation, and I have never seen an infant increase in weight so rapidly as he has done."
"H. E. TRESTRAIL, F.R.C.S., M.R.C.P."

Full Directions accompany each Tin. Price 6d., 1s., 2s., 5s., and 10s. Sold everywhere.

Allen & Hanburys,   Plough Court, Lombard
                        Street, E.C.

West End House:—VERE STREET, CAVENDISH SQUARE, W.   Works:—BETHNAL GREEN, E.
Australian Agency:—484, COLLINS STREET, Melbourne.

4　　　　　　　　　　　*ADVERTISEMENTS.*

THE CHURCH HOUSE,

DEAN'S YARD, WESTMINSTER, LONDON, S.W.

The Business House of the Church of England,

President:—THE LORD ARCHBISHOP OF CANTERBURY.

Vice-Presidents:—THE DUKE OF WESTMINSTER, K.G.; THE LORD BISHOP OF LONDON.

WHAT IS THE CHURCH HOUSE?—The "Business House" of the Church of England.
A Building to be used as the chief meeting place for all the various Church bodies, such as the Convocations of Bishops and Clergy, who, with the help of the House of Laymen, consider measures for the good of the Church with a view to action, reform, and progress. The Church House is also to be a Church Office, where records and documents may be stored, books of reference kept, information collected and given, and the increasing business of the Church transacted.

WHY IS A CHURCH HOUSE NEEDED?—
Because of the vast growth of the Church's work. Although it is little known that the great Church of England has no proper accommodation for the above-named purposes and many others, the need has long been keenly felt by those who see most of the Church's business.

THE SITUATION OF THE CHURCH HOUSE.—
The site of the Church House is about an acre in extent, and is on the south side of Dean's Yard, Westminster. Situated in the shadow of the venerable Abbey, quite near to the Houses of Parliament, and in the best part of London, it is at once very central, easily accessible, quiet, and especially suitable owing to its religious and historical associations.

CONDITIONS OF MEMBERSHIP.

1. Membership of the Corporation may be acquired by persons of either sex (being members of the Church of England, or of any Church in full communion therewith) by an Annual Subscription of at least One Guinea.
2. Life Membership may be acquired by a Donation in one sum of at least Ten Guineas.
3. Associates of the Corporation must be recommended by a Member of the Corporation, and pay an Annual Subscription of at least Five Shillings.

Communications should be addressed to the Secretary, SYDNEY W. FLAMANK, Esq., Church House, Dean's Yard, Westminster, S.W.; or to the Organising Secretary, the Rev. J. A. BETTS, Church House, Dean's Yard, Westminster, S.W.

Wm. WOOLLAMS & Co.,

ORIGINAL MAKERS OF

ARTISTIC

WALL-PAPERS,

GUARANTEED FREE FROM ARSENIC.

☞ Specialities for Studios and Picture Galleries.

A large collection of fine old Damask and Chintz Papers.

 Special facilities for Printing Extra Widths and Lengths. Estimates for Private Patterns given.

Sole Address:
110, HIGH STREET (near Manchester Square), LONDON, W.

SPECIAL TERMS FOR EXPORT.

Society for Promoting Christian Knowledge.

THE ROMANCE OF SCIENCE.

TIME. By Professor C. V. Boys, A.R.S.M., F.R.S. [*In preparation.*

OUR SECRET FRIENDS AND FOES. By Professor Percy F. Frankland, F.R.S. With numerous Illustrations, post 8vo., cloth boards. 2s. 6d.

COLOUR. By Captain Abney, F.R.S. With numerous Diagrams, post 8vo., cloth boards. 2s. 6d.

COAL. By Professor R. Meldol. With numerous Diagrams, post 8vo., cloth boards. 2s. 6d.

DISEASES OF PLANTS. By Professor Marshall Ward. With numerous Illustrations, post 8vo., cloth boards. 2s. 6d.

TIME AND TIDE: a Romance of the Moon. Second Edition, Revised. By Sir Robert S. Ball, LL.D., F.R.S., Astronomer-Royal of Ireland. Illustrated, post 8vo., cloth boards. 2s. 6d.

THE STORY OF A TINDER-BOX. By the late Charles Meymott Tidy, M.B.M.S., F.C.S. With numerous Illustrations, post 8vo., cloth boards. 2s.

THE BIRTH AND GROWTH OF WORLDS. A Lecture by Professor Green, M.A., F.R.S. Post 8vo., cloth boards. 1s.

SOAP BUBBLES AND THE FORCES WHICH MOULD THEM. Being a Course of Three Lectures delivered at the London Institution in December, 1889, and January, 1890, before a Juvenile Audience. By C. V. Boys, A.R.S.M., F.R.S. With numerous Diagrams, post 8vo., cloth boards. 2s. 6d.

SPINNING TOPS. The Operatives' Lecture of the British Association Meeting at Leeds, September, 1890. By Professor J. Perry, M.E., D.Sc., F.R.S. With numerous Diagrams, post 8vo., cloth boards. 2s. 6d.

THE MAKING OF FLOWERS. By the Rev. Professor George Henslow, M.A., F.L.S., F.G.S. With several Illustrations, post 8vo., cloth boards. 2s. 6d.

NEW SERIES OF PHOTO-RELIEVO MAPS. (PATENTED.)

[Presenting each region as if in actual relief, and thus affording an accurate picture of the configuration of the earth's surface.]

ENGLAND AND WALES. Size, 56 inches by 46 inches. Mounted on Canvas, roller, and varnished, coloured. 13s.

SOUTH LONDON. Size, 19 inches by 14 inches. Stretching from London Bridge to Caterham, and from Greenwich to Hampton Court.

The importance of teaching geography by beginning in a small centre has been strongly insisted upon by experts. This Map will be useful, therefore, to all the schools in the district embraced, as well as to others.

NO. 2. PHYSICAL CONFIGURATION, Railways, Roads, and Chief Places. 6d.

NORTH LONDON. Size, 19 inches by 14 inches. No. 2. Railways, Roads, and Chief Places. 6d.

SCOTLAND. Size, 19 inches by 14 inches. No. 1. Names of Places and Rivers to be filled in by Scholars. 6d. No. 2. With Rivers and Names of Places. 9d. No. 3. With Names of Places and with County Divisions in Colours. 1s.

ENGLAND AND WALES, EUROPE, AND ASIA. Same size and price.

STAR ATLAS. Gives all the Stars from 1 to 6·5 magnitude between the North Pole and 34° South Declination, and all Nebulæ and Star Clusters which are visible in telescopes of moderate powers. Translated and adapted from the German of Dr. Klein, by the Rev. E. McClure, M.A. New Edition, brought up to date. Imp. 4to. With 18 Charts and 80 pages of Illustrative Letterpress. Cloth boards. 7s. 6d.

∗ It was by this Atlas that Dr. Anderson discovered the new Star in Auriga.

CHRISTINA G. ROSSETTI. — THE FACE OF THE DEEP. A Devotional Commentary on the Apocalypse. Demy 8vo., cloth boards. 7s. 6d.

" The skilfullest divine without a touch of poetry must blunder over the Apocalypse ; and the usual poet without some tincture of divinity, though he can hardly miss its beauties, must be naturally 'désorienté' in it. Miss Rossetti holds both keys. And it is, perhaps, almost more noteworthy in her that, possessing them, she does not stray, as the possessor of both might be thought likely to do, into bypaths of will-worship."—*Saturday Review.*

AUTHOR of "The Chronicles of the Schonberg Cotta Family."— THREE MARTYRS OF THE NINETEENTH CENTURY. Studies from the Lives of Gordon, Livingstone, and Patteson. Crown 8vo., cloth boards. 3s. 6d.

"There is an ample list of authorities, and the clear, large type greatly adds to the pleasure of the reader."— *Saturday Review.*

REV. AUGUSTUS JESSOPP, D.D.—DORIS: An Idyl of Arcady. 18mo., limp cloth. 6d.

London : Northumberland Avenue, Charing Cross, W.C.; 43, Queen Victoria Street, E.C. Brighton : 135, North Street.

6 *ADVERTISEMENTS.*

CARRIAGES INSURED
AGAINST ACCIDENTAL DAMAGE
BY THE
CARRIAGE INSURANCE COMPANY, LIMITED.
Chief Office: 17, PALL MALL EAST, LONDON, S.W.

DIRECTORS.—G. ALAN LOWNDES, Esq., J.P., D.L., Chairman; The Hon. HENRY NOEL; THOMAS FREDERICK HALSEY, Esq., M.P.; Col. the Hon. FRANCIS C. BRIDGMAN, M.P.

Prospectuses, &c., post free on application to the Secretary.

AGENTS WANTED.

Sir HENRY THOMPSON, F.R.C.S., in "Food and Feeding," writes as follows:—"Pure distilled water, re-supplied with atmospheric air by a special process, and then well charged with carbonic acid gas, is now furnished at so reasonable a cost in London as to be within the reach of persons of moderate means. It is almost needless to say that so prepared water is *absolutely pure*, and nothing more safe or wholesome can be employed for drinking purposes,

THE PURE WATER COMPANY'S
SPARKLING PURALIS.
Pure Distilled Water Aerated with Carbon-Oxygen Gas.
THE CHEAPEST and PUREST TABLE WATER.
A Champagne quart costs 2½d.; a Champagne pint, 1½d.

The Company's Specialities and other Waters (including Soda, Seltzer, Lemonade, Home-brewed Ginger Beer, Ginger Ale, Potass, Lime Juice, &c., &c.) may be obtained through any Grocer, Wine Merchant, or Store. Send post-card for name of nearest Agent to
THE PURE WATER CO., LTD., Queen's Road, Battersea Park, London, S.W.

TO THE NOBILITY AND GENTRY.

CANDLES
FOR THE DINNER TABLE.
NOT AFFECTED BY HEAT.
"A Specialité."
CHARLES FARRIS,
Successor to WHITMORE & CRADDOCK,

MAKER of HIGH-CLASS and ECCLESIASTICAL CANDLES.

ESTABLISHED 50 YEARS.

Special Purveyor to the Royal Palaces, &c.
A DETAILED PRICE LIST SENT TO ANY ADDRESS.

81, BISHOPSGATE STREET WITHIN, E.C.

NORTHERN
ASSURANCE CO.

INCOME & FUNDS
(1891.)

Fire Premiums,
£689,000

Life Premiums,
£225,000

Interest,
£162,000

Accumulated
Funds,
£4,057,000

NORTHERN
ASSURANCE CO.

BRANCHES:

BIRMINGHAM.
BRISTOL.
DUBLIN.
DUNDEE.
EDINBURGH
GLASGOW.
LIVERPOOL.
MANCHESTER.
NEWCASTLE.
NOTTINGHAM.
BOSTON, U.S.
CHICAGO.
CINCINNATI.
NEW YORK.
SAN FRANCISCO.
MONTREAL.
MELBOURNE.

HEAD OFFICES—LONDON : 1, Moorgate Street, E.C. ABERDEEN : 1, Union Terrace

LONDON BOARD OF DIRECTORS.

COLONEL ROBERT BARING.
HENRY COSMO ORME BONSOR, ESQ., M.P.
ERNEST CHAPLIN, ESQ.
SIR PHILIP CURRIE, G.C.B.
ALEXANDER PEARSON FLETCHER, ESQ.

ALEXANDER HEUN GOSCHEN, ESQ.
WILLIAM EGERTON HUBBARD, ESQ.
FERDINAND MARSHALL HUTH, ESQ.
HENRY JAMES LUBBOCK, ESQ.
WILLIAM WALKINSHAW, ESQ.

Secretary—H. E. WILSON.
Fire Department—JAS. ROBB, *Manager.*—Life Department—F. LAING, *Actuary.*
General Manager—JAS. VALENTINE.

WRITE TO—

EYRE & SPOTTISWOODE,

East Harding Street, London, E.C.,

FOR

ACTS OF PARLIAMENT,

BLUE BOOKS,

OR ANY

GOVERNMENT PUBLICATIONS.

LIST OF ANY SERIES SENT POST FREE ON RECEIPT OF ADDRESS.

ALSO AGENTS TO THE NEW ZEALAND GOVERNMENT.

PEARS

SOAP   MAKERS,

By Special Appointment

TO HER MAJESTY

THE QUEEN

AND

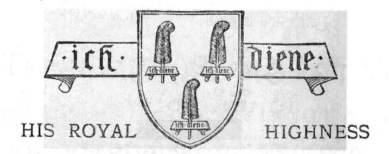

HIS ROYAL   HIGHNESS

THE PRINCE OF WALES.

CPSIA information can be obtained
at www.ICGtesting.com
Printed in the USA
LVHW080117080423
743789LV00004B/254